G000253647

Watford and South West Herts in the Great War

Your Towns and Cities in the Great War

Watford and South West Herts in the Great War

Eugenia Russell and Quentin Russell

Pen & Sword
MILITARY

First published in Great Britain in 2015 by
PEN & SWORD MILITARY
an imprint of
Pen and Sword Books Ltd
47 Church Street
Barnsley
South Yorkshire S70 2AS

Copyright © Eugenia Russell and Quentin Russell, 2015

ISBN 978 1 78346 374 9

The right of Eugenia Russell and Quentin Russell to be identified as the authors of this work has been asserted by them in accordance with the Copyright, Designs and Patents Act 1988.

A CIP record for this book is available from the British Library

All rights reserved. No part of this book may be reproduced or transmitted in any form or by any means, electronic or mechanical including photocopying, recording or by any information storage and retrieval system, without permission from the Publisher in writing.

Printed and bound in England
by CPI Group (UK) Ltd, Croydon, CR0 4YY

Typeset in Times New Roman by Chic Graphics

Pen & Sword Books Ltd incorporates the imprints of
Pen & Sword Archaeology, Atlas, Aviation, Battleground, Discovery, Family History, History, Maritime, Military, Naval, Politics, Railways, Select, Social History, Transport, True Crime, and Claymore Press, Frontline Books, Leo Cooper, Praetorian Press, Remember When, Seaforth Publishing and Wharncliffe.

For a complete list of Pen and Sword titles please contact
Pen and Sword Books Limited
47 Church Street, Barnsley, South Yorkshire, S70 2AS, England
E-mail: enquiries@pen-and-sword.co.uk
Website: www.pen-and-sword.co.uk

Contents

Abbreviations of Awards for Gallantry or Meritorious Service

VC	The Victoria Cross
DSO	The Distinguished Service Order
DSC	The Distinguished Service Cross – Royal Navy
MC	The Military Cross
DFC	Distinguished Flying Cross
AFC	Air Force Cross
DCM	The Distinguished Conduct Medal
MM	The Military Medal
DFM	Distinguished Flying Medal
AFM	Air Force Medal
MSM	The Meritorious Service Medal
MiD	Mentioned in Despatches
	Citation for Gallantry Award

Introduction

Before the War

In retrospect the summer of 1914 is often viewed as the last golden moment of the Edwardian era. With Europe on the brink of total war, Southern England appears frozen in its own imagined idyll; a land where, in Rupert Brooke's 'revered dream', time stood still with 'the church clock at ten to three' and 'honey still for tea'. To the people of Britain the unfolding drama across the Channel seemed far away, as they enjoyed the picnic-perfect weather, the forecast set fair for the coming August Bank Holiday.

Hertfordshire was then a mostly rural county. Life moved to traditional country rhythms and in this world of large estates and country houses, long established hierarchies and customs were largely respected. Even in the towns the aristocratic families and the landed gentry continued to exercise a paternalistic local influence and authority.

On the outskirts of Watford were the Grove, the Georgian residence of the Liberal politician Lord Hyde, the 5th Earl of Clarendon, and Cassiobury Park, the estate of George Capell, the 7th Earl of Essex, with its Tudor House. Both landowners were involved with the affairs of the town. In addition, Gorhambury House, near St Albans, was the Palladian style mansion of Viscount Grimston, the 3rd Earl of Verulam, who had represented St Albans in Parliament. Similarly, Hatfield House, the famous Jacobean seat of the Conservative politician and statesman Viscount Cranbone, the 4th Marquis of Salisbury, dominated the small town.

After the devastation and turmoil of the Great War much of this way of life was no longer viable, and in the democratic new order that followed it soon became a distant memory. The estates were broken up and the country houses sold. The rolling green hills on Hertfordshire's southern border were drawn into the sprawl of Greater London, to be industrialised and subsumed into the suburban world glorified in the poster dreams of 'Metroland'.

During the summer of 1914, change was, in reality, already in the air. There was industrial strife, unrest in Ireland, and the suffragettes were agitating for the vote. Factors such as technological innovation and increased access to its benefits were eating away at the complacency of the establishment. Across Europe, from 1910 onwards war had begun to seem inevitable to many. This appetite for militarism was not universally shared. As the writer and cartoonist Max Beerbohm (1872–1956) prophesied, war would be 'not so much a purge as an additional poison'.

Even in rural areas of Hertfordshire still dominated by the large landowners, social and technological changes were already impacting on the stolid pastoral round of the region. The break up of the large estates had begun, along with the consequent transformation to urban development that became such a feature of the interwar years. Improved transport links with London brought the south of England within range of suburban sprawl. Light industries, particularly those with a metropolitan connection, such as printing and the embryonic British film industry, had begun to flourish – a trend that was to continue at a greater pace after the war.

Transport connections to the capital were by now so superior to those across the county east to west, that some Hertfordshire County Council meetings were held in Holborn, rather than Hertford or St Albans. This transition was driven in part by proximity to London, but also by the growth of Watford itself, which was expanding into the surrounding countryside. By 1901 Watford had become the largest town in the county and its growth prompted nearby Bushey Council to elect to become an urban district in 1906, for fear that the village would become absorbed by its larger neighbour.

In the 1830s Watford's population was a mere 3,000, but by 1914 it had usurped the position of St Albans, which, with its ancient market and abbey, had historically dominated the region. The Diocese of St Albans not only administered the Anglican parishes but it was also a major landholder. In 1877 St Albans underlined its importance when the abbey was elevated into a cathedral and the town was granted city status.

The role reversal was slow in coming. A map of 1849 shows Watford lying between the rivers Gade and Colne, as, in Daniel Defoe's words, still little more than 'a genteel market town, very long, having but one street', and liable to flooding where it crossed marshy land near the Colne. Defoe's description of Watford in his *Tour Through the Whole Island of Great Britain* (1724) was systematically reproduced in pamphlets and tour guides for at least 100 years. Yet, little had changed when David Downer described Watford and neighbouring Bushey in his memoir written during the Great War:

> *Seventy years ago Watford had only one street – High-street – commencing at the Toll Gate at the bottom of the town near the Railway Arches, and crossing the River Colne by a bridge – a much narrower one than the present one, and with a ford at the side for horses and carts to go through, and I expect the town took the name from it of Wet or Whatford. For passing through the toll gate 6d. was charged for a horse and cart and 3d. for a man on horseback. At the end of the garden at Frogmore House, ran a narrow lane (generally full of water), which was the entrance to Bushey Meads. (Recollection, 1916)*

By 1861 the town had grown to a modest 4,385. In the centre of the High Street, near the handsome Parish Church of St Mary the Virgin, (Watford's oldest building, erected in 1230 on an earlier foundation, with the tower added in the fifteenth century), there was a thriving weekly market which traded mainly in corn, local silk and livestock. The produce came from the surrounding landscape; a mixture of arable, pasture and woodland, with numerous hamlets and villages between the small towns. The tradition of holding the market in the High Street lasted until 1928.

The close proximity of fast flowing water had provided the energy for a number of traditional local industries in the town, including silk, paper and cotton mills. Silk production, which Watford had pioneered in the region, was already a thing of the past. The largest silk mill, Rookery Mill, believed to date back to the 1770s, was on the River Colne. Two other mills with which it was connected were horse-

Watford Market during the War. (Hertfordshire Archives)

powered. At their peak, the three mills employed about 500 people, but by 1914 the Rookery Mill had become the Watford Steam Laundry and Dye Works. Waterpower was still important though for Grove Mills on the Gade, bordering Grove Park, and for three cloth working mills on the Colne, to the south-west of Oxhey Hall.

The abundance of water had other uses too. As early as the seventeenth century, the purity of the waters of the River Colne attracted London brewers to the town. Sedgwick's Brewery, believed to date back to around 1655, was located in the lower High Street. The Dyson Brewery, originally established in the 1750s near to St Mary's moved to a larger site opposite. Benskin's Brewery eventually outstripped them all by progressively buying out Dyson's and the other smaller breweries from 1865 onwards, including Sedgwick's in 1923. Benskin's fine brewery house is currently occupied by Watford Museum.

With the improvements in transport networks that took place in the nineteenth century, Watford's proximity to major transport links became increasingly important. Before the coming of the railways, Watford had been a coaching stop on the road to Aylesbury and the North. The coach service from London, which ran until 1886, came to Watford twice a day and took four hours. The journey to St Albans, a mere 5 miles away, took a whole day. The journey to London by boat on the Grand Junction Canal, fully operational since 1805, also took a day.

This all changed when George Stephenson opened the first railway from Liverpool to Manchester in 1830, in order to facilitate the speedy delivery of raw cotton from Liverpool harbour to the water-powered cotton mills at Manchester and then back for export. Once Stephenson had persuaded Parliament that steam trains were the future, the demand for passenger trains grew dramatically, if rather unexpectedly.

The impact of Stephenson's innovation was soon felt in Watford, where Josiah Conder, the prominent abolitionist intellectual and editor of the *Congregational Hymn Book* (1836), noted:

> *Everybody knows where Watford is; for it is a station on the North-Western Railway, and everybody has travelled by the North-Western Railway. Everybody knows how the railway sweeps in a quarter-circle round the quiet little town ...*

The London and Birmingham Railway (later part of the London and North Western), built by Robert Stevenson, George's son, passed through Watford. The first intercity line into London, the initial stretch between Euston and Boxmoor (Hemel Hempstead) was opened in July 1837, the final stretches being completed the following year. The first London train ran into Birmingham on 17 September 1838.

The line was not built without opposition, though. Public protest meetings had been held along the proposed route through West Hertfordshire, most notably at Berkhampstead and Watford. The construction was opposed by influential local landowners, including the Earl of Essex and the Earl of Clarendon, who wanted to protect their estates. The anatomist, Sir Ashley Paston Cooper, whose Gadebridge House was just outside Hemel Hempstead, was influential enough to ensure that the residents of the town had no station of their own, but had to travel to nearby Boxmoor instead.

In Watford, the station (no longer in use) was initially situated north of St Albans Road. Today's mainline station, Watford Junction, situated south of the road, was an additional station on the mainline created in 1858 as a link to St Albans. As in Hemel Hempstead, the station was located at a distance from the High Street to accommodate the complaints from the local residents. Rebuilt in 1909, it played a major role in the town's expansion programme and branch lines to St Albans and Rickmansworth increased Watford's importance.

The London and North Western (L&NWR) also became a major employer in the area, with the influx of railway workers contributing to population growth: 500 of the 1,500 men working on the railways in the 1800s lived in Watford, many of them in newly built homes near St Mary's. The opening of Willesden Junction Station in 1866, a major interchange connecting passenger and goods lines from the north and the west of London with Euston and the London docks, as well as destinations south of the Thames, was a further boost to the town.

With the growth in population came a desire for leisure activities. A measure of the extent to which Watford had become a thriving centre was the establishment of sports clubs. Watford Rovers Football Club was founded in 1881. Between 1890 and 1896, Lord Clarendon, a keen sportsman, became a member of the Football Committee of the club, (now termed the West Hertfordshire Sports Club), and he chaired some of the meetings. By the late 1890s the club had begun to move from a purely amateur membership to including paid professionals. It merged in 1898 with another local club, Watford St Mary's, to become Watford Football Club and went on to play in the Southern League.

This was a period of rapid growth for the town. By 1891 the population had reached 17,063, growing to 29,329 by 1901 and 40,939 by 1911. Initially Watford's rapid growth was related more to its desirability as a residential area rather than to industry. For those who wanted to escape from London for picturesque countryside and clean air Watford and its environs, renowned for their leafy surroundings and orchards, were a suitable place to live and work. The rise of commuting culture created the ideal of the modern suburb, which Watford epitomized. Amazingly, to increase the volume of suburban traffic, in the 1870s the L&NWR offered free season tickets lasting for twenty-one years to certain buyers of properties in the area.

Watford was now experiencing what historians call a 'restrained' revolution, as opposed to the heavy-duty, full-on industrial revolution which had occurred in the North. By the turn of the century, the upkeep for the country residences of the gentry was becoming prohibitively by expensive and parts of the old estates began to be sold off – including the Earl of Essex's Cassiobury Park in 1897 – to be replaced by villas, terraced houses, shops and factories. The shift to industry began in earnest during this period, creating a new Watford which had the advantage of a separation between housing and industrial areas, creating a more pleasant living environment.

The availability and comparative cheapness of the land to the west and east of the town, and the good railway facilities, resulted in the building of a number of factories and works: Fowler's Jam Company, the Watford Manufacturing Co. (makers of Dr. Tibbles' cocoa, chocolates and food products), engineering works, a cold storage company, and large works for colour printing and engraving. Dr Tibbles' Vi-Cocoa Factory, built in 1899 had its own railway siding, probably pre-dating Watford North Station.

A large number of the employees of the L&NWR were housed near to the main railway station in the Callowland district, then known as Watford New Town. The 1901 census records that only 10 per cent of the heads of households in Leavesden Road were born in Watford. St Andrews, the first Anglican church to be built in Watford since the Reformation, was founded in 1853 in response to this growth in the population. The church's links to the railway were marked by an annual street procession and service on a Sunday in June organized by the local branch of the Railwaymen's Union, in aid of their Widows and Orphans Fund. This was discontinued after 1914.

Printing had been established in the area as early as 1816. There were a number of locally produced newspapers, with the most successful proving to be the *Watford Observer*, which is still in operation today. Samuel Peacock, the son of John Peacock, a bookbinder who had founded a printworks in 1824, brought out *The Watford Observer and General Advertiser for Watford, Bushey and Rickmansworth* on 24 January 1863. The first issue, consisting of three pages of national and one page of local news, contained the paper's ethos that, however unpopular this might prove, it would expose 'social injustice and [stand] for the people'. The paper stayed in the ownership of the Peacock family until 1957.

In all, there were an impressive eight printing houses in Watford by 1878. Over the years a number of printing companies were absorbed into others. By the 1900s Bemrose Dalziel, based in the New Town, was at the forefront of multi-colour printing, producing outstanding chromolithographs for such publications as *Vanity Fair*, while nearby Waterlow and Sons was printing paper currency. In 1914 photogravure specialists André & Sleigh and the Bushey Colour Press, both in Bushey, were acquired by the Anglo Engraving Co. of London, becoming André, Sleigh & Anglo Ltd. and with Menpes Printing and Engraving Co. of Whippendale Road, Watford; they were all eventually absorbed by the Sun Engraving Co. Ltd. (later Sun Printers) in 1919.

By 1914 these industries were being supplemented by machine and tool-making, and the manufacture of motor vehicle parts. The hostilities of 1914 to 1918 did not impede this industrial growth and by 1921 the town's population had grown to 56,802. In fact Watford's industrial importance increased between the wars and, with the arrival of the famous Odhams Press in 1954, it became a major centre of the printing industry. Until the 1960s printing made Watford one of the five richest towns in England.

On the eve of the Great War, Watford's growth had taken in the nearby hamlet of Cassio to the north and joined it to Leavesden to the north-east and Oxhey, on the Middlesex border. To the east, today's suburb of Garston on the St Albans Road was still a small village. By 1908, to the north a residential area was already in existence, bounded by Hempstead Road on the west and the railway on the east. It was described by William Page in his *History of the County of Hertfordshire* (1908) as well timbered, with 'many pleasant residences, with large gardens and grounds, mostly occupied by gentlemen engaged in business in London'.

Near the centre of Watford, The Girls' Grammar School had taken over a new site in Lady's Close in 1907, while the present Boys' Grammar School buildings were opened in 1912 on former landscaped parkland purchased from the Cassiobury Park Estate. In 1914 The Great Central Railway took an additional five and a half acres of the estate for development. In Leavesden, dominating the village on adjacent sites, were the Metropolitan Asylum for Imbeciles, opened in 1870 with accommodation for 2,000 inmates, and the St Pancras Industrial School for 500 pauper children from London. In 1915 Leavesden Asylum infirmary became a centre for dealing with cases of trachoma. On land near Watford Junction Station the (East) London Orphan Asylum had opened a school in 1871, which was renamed the London Orphan School in 1915.

Around 1900, available farmland led to further expansion to the west of the town. The construction of the rail link to Croxley Green in 1912 (now defunct) encouraged industrial use and most of the houses built there were small and affordable, attracting a large number of workers employed in London. During this period the town's infrastructure was improved and its health and educational services expanded to meet the growing demands. There were still slum districts, but they were not considered as bad as those in St Albans or Hitchin.

The Watford Union Workhouse was then in Colney Butts, near the cemetery in what is now Vicarage Road. From 1904, to protect inhabitants from potential prejudice or any disadvantage in later life, the birth certificates for those born in the Workhouse gave its address merely as '60 Vicarage Road, Watford'. After 1929, the workhouse changed its name to Shrodells Public Assistance Institution and the introduction of the National Health Service in 1948 led to another name change, to Watford General Hospital.

A little further out of town was the Watford and District Isolation Hospital in Tolpits Lane, opened in 1896 to cater for sufferers from infectious diseases. Previously such cases amongst the poor had been dealt within the Workhouse Infirmary or the Pest House, or not at all. The hospital was not required to treat venereal disease patients, who still went to the Workhouse, or tuberculosis sufferers, who went to special sanatoriums. Built on land provided by the Earl of Essex, the Isolation Hospital had two wards and two isolation blocks with a capacity for 42 beds. In 1904 this was enlarged to 64 beds.

To the south of Watford, on the road to London and bordering Middlesex, was Bushey (estimated population of 7,680 in 1914) itself made up of small hamlets: Great Bushey, Little Bushey, Bushey Heath, Bushey Hartsbourne – which were in danger of joining together and linking Watford to London as one urban sprawl. Beyond Bushey Arches, where the railway line sweeps majestically across the shallow valley of the Colne, by the old tollgate marking the edge of Watford, was 'New Bushey', the district adjoining Bushey Station. This area had been developed from the 1880s onwards, and by 1908 William Page described it as consisting of 'modern houses mostly occupied by those whose work takes them daily to London'. The Bushey Grove estate on the north side of the London Road was also undergoing development, with streets being laid out and suburban villas erected.

Other big estates (including the Little Bushey Estate) were in the process of being split up for building plots. The area was not merely residential, though. In 1905, just across the tracks from Watford, Blyth and Platt, boot and polish manufacturers, had opened their Solar Works on Greatham Road. This became the home of their Cobra brand polish. By 1914 the company was enjoying a period of great success. A large overseas consignment of over 700,000 tins and bottles weighing 40 tons and valued at £5,500 required nearly fifty railway lorries to transport. An article in the *Watford Observer* claimed that even this figure was about to be surpassed. The factory employed a large number of young women in their filling and foiling rooms, where one employee on the filling line was capable of filling 20,000 tins per hour.

In 'picturesque' Bushey, Page records the influence of Herkomer's Art School as still hanging over the village, with its 'colony of artists' and numerous studios. This artistic ambiance carried through into the designs of many of the houses, the most impressive of which was Lululand, the large Bavarian style home of the painter Sir Hubert von Herkomer (1849–1914). Herkomer kept up his connections with his native Bavaria and his career was an example of the close cultural ties that existed between Britain and Germany before the First World War. By this time his school had closed (in 1904) and Herkomer had turned his considerable energies to film-making; his Bushey Film Studios opened in 1913. His school was replaced by the Bushey Art School, run by his former pupil and renowned animal artist, Lucy Kemp Welch.

Herkomer, who is buried in St James's Churchyard, died just before the outbreak of war, so he was saved the trauma of the anti-German backlash that would follow. His third wife, Margaret, Lady Herkomer, (the sister of his second wife, Lulu Griffiths, after whom the house was named), moved out of Lululand to another property nearby.

The open spaces of Bushey were dotted with a number of large, and sometimes extravagant, houses, in addition to institutions like The Royal Masonic School for Boys (now a residential development), the Caledonian Asylum (today's Purcell School) and St Margaret's Clergy Orphan School for Girls, which were significant landmarks. The main road to London had become busy enough for the parishioners of St

Lucy Kemp-Welch's house, Bushey.

Peter's Church, Bushey Heath, to complain that the traffic noise was disturbing Sunday worship. A petrol station and garage established on the High Street since 1911 (demolished in 2014) attested to its significant use by motorcars.

The influence of waterpower on the industrial fabric of the Watford area was particularly apparent to the north of the town, where the influence of London was less strongly felt. On the way to Hemel Hempstead, then still a small market town, were a number of villages and small hamlets, notably Abbots Langley, King's Langley and Apsley End, with several mills. The River Gade, shadowed by the Grand Union Canal, passes through these on its way to Watford and Rickmansworth.

John Dickinson & Co, 'the large envelope and card manufacturers', makers of the Lion brand stationary (1910) and the company that acquired Basildon Bond in 1918, were founded in Apsley, near Hemel Hempstead. Their mills nearby and at Croxley were the largest in the country, employing 3,000 people. As well as Apsley Mills, they owned Home Park Paper Mills, where many of the inhabitants of King's Langley worked, plus the Nash Paper Mill and Hunton Mill near Abbots Langley. John Dickinson had been a pioneer in paper-making, and Jean Rennard claims that much the success of the Hertfordshire paper industry was due to his 'dynamic character and inventive mind', which:

> *enabled him to gain advantage over the smaller mills, until only his mills remained ... After 1908 the story of the Hertfordshire paper industry is that of John Dickinson & Co., Ltd.*

But the local economy was not only about paper. At Apsley, Messrs, Kent & Sons had recently founded a large brush factory and the inhabitants of Abbots Langley, who were mainly engaged in agriculture, also found employment in connection with the Metropolitan District Asylum at Leavesden close by.

To the north-east of Watford, towards St Albans, was an agricultural belt in the midst of which was Brickett Wood, where Henry and Frederick Grey had developed the Woodside Retreat, on land they had acquired from 1887, as a family fairground attraction. By 1914 it had become extremely popular, with 5,000 teas being served daily, but this success was curtailed when it was requisitioned as a wartime camp. To the east, the Midland Railway out of St Pancras served a number of villages along the route of Watling Street, enabling gentlemen well-heeled enough to have small estates within the area around Radlett and Shenley, to pursue their commercial interests in the City.

The commute to London began with the opening of the station at Radlett on 1 October 1868. The improved train service and the development of part of the Kendals and Aldenham Lodge Estates near to the station brought with it an increase in the suburban population. Similarly, there was comparable growth around the stations at Elstree and Borehamwood.

Away from the railway, the population was still made up of farmers and agricultural labourers. Complementing the main activity of farming, much pasture, gravel and sand was worked in places for industrial purposes. Wellington and Ward, makers of photographic paper, and The Panama Hat Company which flourished in Borehamwood during this time, added some diversity. It was here that, in 1914, the Neptune Film Company opened its studio – a foretaste of things to come.

To the west, the market town of Rickmansworth was already connected to Watford by the Grand Union Canal, by way of Croxley and Chorleywood. Situated at the confluence of the Rivers Colne, Gade and Chess, it was the terminus of a branch of the London and North West Railway from Watford which opened in 1862. The line was initially the brainchild of Lord Ebury, who had his estate at nearby Moor Park, and was designed to bring growth to the town, but it merely contributed to the further growth of its larger neighbour.

The line has a troubled history; the station at Croxley Green is said to have been burned down by suffragettes in 1913, and it struggled financially. Passenger traffic ceased in the 1950s, although some freight was carried into the 1980s. To the north-west of Rickmansworth, bordering Buckinghamshire, down narrow lanes and nestling amidst woodland and pasture, lay the village of Sarratt and its surrounding hamlets. Cherry orchards were a particular feature of the village and they provided extra income for a population reliant upon corn and roots.

The Metropolitan Railway had reached Rickmansworth and Chorleywood in 1887, bringing in its wake a spate of residential development in the midst of woodland and arable farmland. The cultivation of watercress beds along the banks of the three rivers provided an important industry. The rivers also furnished the power for numerous mills in the area. At their confluence, just outside Rickmansworth, was a corn mill and in the town there was a mineral water works (Messrs Franklin & Sons) and the Uxbridge Valley Water Works, converted from an old paper mill. John Dickinson's thriving Croxley Paper Mills, built in 1830, was on the River Gade and Peter Clutterbuck J.P. owned paper mills at Mill End on the Colne and at Scots Bridge on the Chess. At Croxley Green, the International Photo Printing Syndicate Limited was based in a former paper mill.

Historically, this area has had a long Nonconformist and Quaker tradition. At Heronsgate, south-west of Chorleywood, Feargus O'Connor, MP, 'Chartist, idealist and social reformer' (as described by the inscription on the Blue Plaque that honours him), bought an estate in 1847. The land was divided into smallholdings and let to the subscribers to his 'National Land Company', founded in 1845 to help working-class people satisfy the landholding requirement to gain a vote in county seats. The subsequent settlement became briefly known as O'Connorsville, but despite the popularity of the plan with the working people who subscribed to it and to other estates bought by the company, hoping they would be able to live an idyllic country life, the political élite mobilized against it and the company was made illegal in 1848.

In the weeks prior to outbreak of war in 1914, the local press showed little interest in the unfolding political situation that would soon define a generation. Summer was in full swing with holiday sales in the shops, agricultural and horticultural shows, annual works outings and cricket matches. A flower show was being held in the grounds of Bushey House; Thomas and Co. Ltd. employees were off to enjoy the weather, while a team from Dickinson's London House was playing the Croxley Mills team at cricket in Croxley Green. Minor counties cricket was being contested at Bushey by Hertfordshire against Norfolk, and the West Herts Tennis Tournament was staging its finals in Watford.

The town's cinemas, the Electric Coliseum and the Central Hall Picture House, were doing brisk business and the Palace Theatre was staging *Little Miss Ragtime,* a musical comedy, followed by *A Messenger from Mars*, a production that promised 'Comedy – Pathos – Mysticism'. It was August Bank Holiday, and the Territorials were under canvas at Ashridge Park, an estate belonging to Baron Brownlow near Berkhampstead.

CHAPTER 1

The Military

Mobilization

Apparently, we were at peace with the world ... most people had arranged or were looking forward to their holidays ... And then came the sudden bolt from the blue and the whole of Europe sprang to arms ... August 4th is one of those momentous dates in our nation's history; the day on which, in the cause of honour, liberty and righteousness, we declared war against Germany ... All able-bodied unmarried men between the ages of eighteen and thirty years should volunteer for service.
(Vicar A.H. Parnell, St Lawrence Church, *Parish Magazine*, Abbots Langley, September 1914.)

At 11.00pm on 4 August 1914, a warm Tuesday night, the Prime Minister Herbert Asquith's ultimatum requesting Germany to respect Belgian neutrality expired. Germany marched into Belgium and Britain was at war. The 'Great War' that followed would be devastating and its consequences were to be felt worldwide.

The following morning, the centre of Watford was filled with the sounds and sights of military activity, as Lieutenant Palmer of the Watford Territorial Infantry mustered his one hundred men outside the Clarendon Hall, all looking, according to the *Watford Illustrated*, 'very fit' and tanned. They had just returned from training at Ashridge Park, Berkhamsted, and were to proceed from Watford to headquarters in Hertford. Meanwhile, Major G.R. Holland and his three officers were

Soldiers marching through Watford. (Hertfordshire Archives)

parading the Watford Artillery, 2nd Hertfordshire Brigade, comprising 174 non-commissioned officers and men, and the Hertfordshire Yeomanry was gathering under the command of Major Wyld, with five other officers. The Yeomanry had also been rushed back from training in Northumberland over the weekend. They formed part of the Eastern Mounted Brigade with its HQ at Hertford; A, B, C and D Squadrons being attached for training at Watford, Hertford, St Albans, and High Barnet.

The Regular Army and Reservists were mobilized first and within days were on their way to France as part of the 150,000 strong British Expeditionary Force (BEF). The Watford Company of the 1st Hertfordshire Regiment left Clarendon Hall that day to join the Battalion at Hertford. The *Watford Illustrated* (29 August 1914) reported that over half of the Battalion had volunteered for foreign service and 'during their marches from town to town they have been treated by the inhabitants in the most hospitable manner, having as

The Watford Company marching from Clarendon Hall. (Watford Illustrated, 13 August 1914)

much fruit, etc. as they wanted.' They arrived in France on 6 November and went on to serve throughout the War on the Western Front, most notably at Ypres, Loos and the Somme as 'one of the finest fighting regiments in the whole of the forces of the British Empire.'

Mounted and artillery units needed more time to get organized. In the following days government horse buyers and officers from the Artillery and Yeomanry were busy scouring the neighbourhood for horses, before leaving Watford on the Saturday for their war stations in Essex. The requisitioning of horses was an early sign of how the War was to impact on the local population. Horses were still in general use and some were taken from pubs, for example the Rose & Crown Hotel in Watford High Street and the Horse & Chains in Bushey.

Once the horses had been examined and passed by a vet, they were branded on one hoof and the owner was offered compensation, which was not to everyone's satisfaction. The landlord of the Horse & Chains was unhappy with the replacement horses he received, while his neighbour, the artist Lucy Kemp-Welch, was relieved that her own horse, Black Prince, given to her by Lord Robert Baden Powell, was not taken. It loathed soldiers and was notoriously afraid of gunfire, so this was probably just as well. Owners of horses could appeal to County Hall if they thought they had not been offered a fair price.

The Hertfordshire Yeomanry had been formed in response to the threat of French invasion in the 1790s. Retained during peacetime, a century later it provided volunteer mounted troops for service in the Boer War. In the extensive reorganization of Britain's Auxiliary forces in 1908 the Yeomanry was incorporated into the Territorial Force, the predecessor of today's Territorial Army. After mobilization it was moved to war stations in East Anglia, where it was split in two. The 1/1 (First Line Regiment) Hertfordshire Yeomanry was the fighting arm and the 2/1 (Second Line) remained as a 'home service' unit based in Hertford throughout the war.

The 1/1 became part of the Eastern Mounted Brigade and by September was stationed in Egypt. From there they were dispatched to take part in the infamous Gallipoli débâcle, returning to Egypt in December 1915, having suffered significant casualties. In 1916 the Regiment was split up again: 'A' Squadron went to Palestine and 'D' Squadron to Mesopotamia, where they participated in the fall of Baghdad. In 1917 they were attached to the 15th Indian Division, and in May 1918 were on communication duties with the North Persia Force. The 2/1 did not see action, although they did supply drafts of fit troops for service in France in 1917. A 3/1 was formed in 1915, which also remained at home until it was absorbed by the 6th Reserve Cavalry Regiment in February 1917.

As the local regiments left for the Front a number of other regiments would take their place over the coming weeks, turning the region into something of a military zone. The mobilization of the army prior to its deployment meant that large numbers of troops had to be billeted on the local population and towns turned into bases, with parks and recreation areas used as training grounds.

The rural areas offered opportunities for military exercises and Watford itself was blessed with a number of open spaces that were ideal for drill purposes. There was already a rifle range of 1,000 yards in Cassiobury Park and from the start local rifle clubs played a role in providing training. The Watford Miniature Rifle Club, the Oxhey Rifle Club and the Bushey and District Rifle Club all opened their facilities to non-members. The Watford Football Club Management 'arranged

The Royal Field Artillery (Territorial Force) in Cassiobury Park. (Watford Illustrated, 20 March 1915)

for their men to devote Tuesday and Thursday afternoon to rifle practice.'

By March 1915, the *Watford Illustrated* was able to publish photographs of the Artillery exercising in Cassiobury Park. Their Gun Park became something of an attraction, with thousands of people turning up on a Sunday to see the men and horses training. The park also provided plenty of space to dig trenches.

Cassiobury Park. (*Watford Illustrated*, 20 March 1915)

Over the coming weeks numerous regiments passed through the area and the local press followed the comings and goings with great interest. The *Watford Illustrated* delighted in showing troops marching through the local streets and drilling in the open spaces on what was then the edge of town, at the Harebreaks off St Albans Road.

The newspaper also reported the arrival of the 2nd London Division of the Royal Field Artillery on 22 August 1914, from their summer camp on Salisbury Plain. Part of the Territorial Force, the 5th and 6th London Artillery Brigades were based at Berkhamsted, Hemel Hempstead and Kings Langley, and their training exercises took them

Troops drilling at the Harebreaks, 1916. (Hertfordshire Archives)

as far afield as Sarratt and Chorleywood. In Chorleywood the common was dug with trenches, a live range established (despite opposition from the council and a number of serious accidents) and a hut built for a bombing school.

The artillery stayed in Hemel Hempstead until March 1915, before being sent to France. From March to May 1915, the 600 soldiers and 500 horses with gun carriages of the 3rd London Brigade were stationed in Rickmansworth. The Inns of Court Officers Training Corps were based at Berkhamsted. The City of London Regiment, also known as the Royal Fusiliers, The Middlesex Regiment, the Civil Service Rifles, The Isle of Wight Rifles, The 1/8 Hampshire Regiment and The Sherwood Foresters, were all based locally at various times throughout the War.

When the London Scottish left Watford for France on 15 September, the local people gave them a warm send off, virtually emptying the shops to buy them gifts of tobacco and other trifles. Yet, in his diary Lieutenant Colonel Edwin Henry Collen expressed anxiety at seeing them leave, believing it was too soon and that they were still raw after such a brief spell of training.

The Isle of Wight Rifles marching out of Cassiobury Park, Watford, in 1915 prior to embarkation to Gallipoli. (Courtesy of the Isle of Wight Family History Society)

Soldiers of the Isle of Wight Rifles, probably at Cassiobury Park, during training. (Courtesy of the Isle of Wight Family History Society)

The London Scottish. (*Watford Illustrated*, 22 August 1914)

For six weeks they carried out duties behind the lines, but then on 31 October 1915 they were thrown into the heat of battle on the ridge at Wytschaete, near Ypres. The London Scottish showed their inexperience when they rushed headlong into the fray, determined to prove to the Regulars what the Territorials could do. But they had misread the situation and found themselves surrounded and overwhelmed by intense fire from all sides. The British press praised their courage, while carefully drawing a veil over the casualties sustained and the foolhardiness of this action. Of the 750 men who had attacked, 345 were killed, wounded or missing by the following day.

Recruitment

When hostilities began Britain had a relatively small professional army made up, unlike those of the other major powers, of volunteers. This army, less than half the size of the German and French armies, was never going to be adequate to meet the demands of a full-scale land war. Within the first week of war, Lord Kitchener, the newly appointed Secretary of State for War, launched the 'Call to Arms' for his New

Army, encouraging men aged between nineteen and forty-two to join the Special Reserves, a part-time force similar to the Territorials.

The famous poster of Kitchener looking the viewer in the eye and pointing his finger, alongside the caption, 'Your country needs you', was part of a massive nationwide recruitment campaign. In Watford, Clarendon Hall was used as the main recruitment venue. Also known as the Agricultural Hall, it was situated in Clarendon Road and used as a Drill Hall by the Hertfordshire Yeomanry and the 2nd Hertfordshire Battery. Later, the 4th East Anglian Brigade Royal Field Artillery was to make it a headquarters and A and G Companies of the 2nd (Hertfordshire) Volunteer Battalion and the Bedfordshire Regiment were based there. There were close ties between the Hertfordshire and Bedfordshire Regiments and many local men served in the Bedfordshire Regiment.

There were a number of other Drill Halls around the county and close by at Hemel Hempstead and St Albans, supplemented by smaller Drill Stations at London Colney and Chorleywood. The Drill Hall in Chorleywood House Estate, Rickmansworth Road, was initially erected by the artist Lady Ela Russell, a relative of the Duke of Bedford, for her Rifle Club. In 1913 the hall was used by D Company of the Hertfordshire Regiment, which was based in Watford, as an outlying drill station. In 1915 it became an Auxiliary Hospital.

In August 1914, Lord Hyde, the son of the Earl of Clarendon, rushed back to Watford with his wife from their fruit farm in Toronto, as the *Watford Illustrated* reported, in order to relieve 'the distress that must follow'. Lord Hyde had emigrated to Canada to distance himself from his dominating father, but the call to duty was something that he felt strongly. Despite being unfit for active service, the result of breaking his hip at Eton, he joined the Hertfordshire Volunteer Regiment and served as temporary Lieutenant Colonel and County Commandant (1916–1920). After the war, in 1922, he became mayor of Watford.

His father likewise threw himself heavily into recruitment meetings held both in halls and the open air. Lord Clarendon (1846–October 1914) had been ADC to Queen Victoria and later King Edward VII, with whom he was on friendly terms. The King had visited the family residence at Grove House on the outskirts of Watford on a number of occasions. Clarendon, who 'was very involved with the progress and welfare of the town', was Lord Lieutenant of Hertfordshire and

Lieutenant Colonel of the Hertfordshire Yeomanry. By this time he was in poor health, but despite this, when he attended a drill by the St John's Ambulance Brigade at the St John's Hall, he still managed to deliver some stirring words of encouragement. He died soon afterwards.

On 29 August the *Watford Observer* carried a letter warning that few men understood the true reasons for the War and therefore they were in need of a motivating sermon. A week later, the *Watford Illustrated* reprinted an appeal carried by the *London Daily Express* written by Major H. Page Croft, of the 1st Battalion, Herts Regiment. In the conclusion of his appeal Croft addressed the nation's women:

> *My last word is to our women, who have never failed. In your hearts you know you will despise your sons if they falter now, and yet your visible tears and your love may hold them back. Yours is the nobler, harder part, for you must encourage them and spur them on.* **Women of Britain, do not fail. God and His Angels will comfort you.**

By early 1915 his sentiments were being echoed in a national poster campaign run by the Parliamentary Recruiting Committee – 'Women of Britain say – Go!'. Aimed particularly at the patriotic sensibilities of middle class women, it portrays a nostalgic, pastoral image of the country with green rolling hills.

In September, some prominent figures leant their support to a concerted recruitment drive at Clarendon Hall. Lord Charles Beresford, retired Admiral and MP for Portsmouth, thought by many to be the embodiment of the British bulldog and often accompanied by one, was the main speaker. Alongside him was Lady Iris Capell, daughter of the Earl of Essex, who pinned a rosette on the lapel of each recruit. The *Watford Illustrated* (5 September 1914) reported that 150 recruits had enrolled in the past week and the total number of recruits had reached 400, equalling recruits throughout the rest of the county, but this was still not enough.

The exhortations continued, using every means possible. Two weeks later the *Watford Illustrated* reported on a 'Great Meeting of Recruitment', again held at Clarendon Hall, featuring an appeal led by 'famous actresses'. Proceedings opened with the 'National Hymns of the Allies' and it was emphasized that 'no nation entered into a war

Recruitment poster by E.V. Kealey, 1915.
(Library of Congress)

with a clearer conscience and a more rightful cause than England on this occasion.' During the meeting the outspoken Miss Lena Ashwell, who went on to pioneer concerts for the troops at the Front, outlined a scheme for women's employment in jobs such as bus driving, conducting and as special constables, to the displeasure of the editor of the paper, who preferred the 'more humorous vein' of the next speaker, Miss Constance Collier.

Meanwhile, in Rickmansworth, for the town's big recruitment drives throughout 1915 the organisers enlisted the support of the local dignitary, ex-member of parliament for Westminster, former Life Guard and Captain of the Cheshire Yeomanry and MCC cricketer, Robert Grosvenor, Lord Elbury, of nearby Moor Park.

The *Watford Observer* launched a 'Local Patriotic Roll', giving the names and location in South West Hertfordshire of those who had joined up. In the first weeks the numbers were:

Sarratt	28
Chipperfield	12
Chorleywood	6
Croxley Green	9
Northwood	2
Kings Langley	38
Hunton Bridge	2
Bushey	28
Bovington	9
Watford	373

On 22 September, Chorleywood Council started its own roll, by which time the number of men serving had grown to eighty-four. All possible means of encouragement were deployed. Mrs Amy Brooke of Bushey was moved to write two recruitment songs in 1915: 'Gallant Belgium' and 'Now Step Along You Khaki Boys'. All these efforts soon bore fruit. In Abbots Langley there were 147 men serving in 1914, 238 in 1915, 343 in 1916 and 440 by 1917. Of these, six were killed in the first year, eleven by the end of 1915, twenty-six in 1916, forty-seven in 1917, and a further twenty-one were disabled due to severe wounds.

Whole groups of men responded to the Call together, with a significant impact for those left behind. In 1915 twenty Watford men enlisted from the twenty-seven houses of one single street, Cross Street. As the memorials show, by the end of the War even the smallest villages had supplied men for the army.

While on the march at the Front, the Hertfordshire Territorials sang new words to the Wesleyan hymn 'Jesu, Lover of my Soul', a reflection of the strong Nonconformist following in the region. The words incorporated the names of several Gade Valley villages:

> *At the front of Flanders*
> *Sing the Hertshire men*
> *Songs they learnt on Sundays,*
> *In the Hertshire glen:*
> *Songs they sang at Apsley,*
> *Hempstead, and Boxmoor,*
> *Or within the Langleys,*
> *On the schoolroom floor.*

Still the schools are standing,
And the songs are sung
By the little children
Where no shells are flung:
And a prayer is offered
For the boys of old,
Fighting now in Flanders
In the trenches cold.

Recruitment also took place within local firms. At the outbreak of war, men from the paper mills were eager conscripts. The diary of John Dickinson's Home Park Mill at Kings Langley records:

Our men went so willingly that it was rather a question of restraining indispensable men from volunteering than of urging any of our men to go. The retreat from Mons [23 August to 5 September 1914] *had its effect on our men as on the whole of our countrymen and reverses only increased the number of those who felt it their duty to enlist.*

The total number of men to enlist from Dickinson's was 1,604. Those who remained were engaged in making trench mortar bombs. The whole factory, therefore, became dedicated to the war effort. By the end of the War, the mill had lost thirteen former employees.

Men from all walks of life enlisted, from the well-known figure of the assistant manager of The Palace Theatre, who joined the Hertfordshire Yeomanry and left for foreign service, to all but two of the staff from Berkhamsted Golf Club, whose jobs were kept open for them and their dependants looked after.

In May 1915 the Hertfordshire Volunteer Regiment was formed. At its peak the regiment was 2,500 strong and volunteers had to provide their own Lovat Green (a type of bluish green tweed) uniforms until 1918, when they were re-designated into the Volunteer Battalions, Hertfordshire Regiment, and issued with khaki uniforms. Throughout the country these local volunteer corps were established to supplement the army in the event of a German invasion. The Government maintained an uneasy relationship with these units, reluctant to acknowledge their services until shortage of manpower forced their

Watford and Bushey Volunteer Corps. (Hertfordshire Archives)

hand. In the spring of 1916 they recognized the need to regulate these groups into a Volunteer Training Corps (VTC), their units making up the Volunteer Force, a forerunner of the Second World War Home Guard.

Not all men from the area served in the same or even local regiments. For instance, on 24 October 1914, the brothers Cecil, aged twenty-five, and Julian Smeathman, aged twenty-six, from South Hill, Hemel Hempstead, died whilst serving with the 1st Battalion, the Leicestershire Regiment and 55th Field Company Royal Engineers respectively, both with the rank of Lieutenant. Julian had been married barely a month before he died. Cecil is buried in Bailleul Communal Cemetery, while Julian has no known grave and is commemorated on the Menin Gate Memorial to the Missing in Ypres.

Similarly, two brothers from Tucker Street, Watford, Henry and Joseph Batchelor, were in the 3rd Dragoon Guards and both died shortly after on 31 October, aged twenty-eight and twenty-nine. Joseph was married and living in North Kensington, London. They have no known graves and are both commemorated on the Menin Gate Memorial.

Ernest Farmer, an agricultural labourer and shepherd, who lived at Bushey Hall Farm Cottages, Bushey Mill Lane, enlisted as a Private with the Northamptonshire Regiment. He served in France and Flanders and was killed in action on 17 February 1917, on the Somme. Like Farmer, Lieutenant Arthur Langton Airy also served in the Northamptonshire Regiment. A former Herkomer Art School student, his death was commemorated in the parish magazine, although he had recently been living in Worthing. The son of a doctor and grandson of Sir George Biddell Airy, Astronomer Royal from 1835 to 1881, he had already seen service in the Boer War. Airy enlisted in the Northamptonshire Regiment in October 1914 and was killed in action in Cuinchy in France on 11 January 1915, aged thirty-nine. He has no known grave. His sister Anna was one of the first women to be commissioned as a war artist.

Herkomer's Art School had been closed for ten years by the outbreak of the War, but a number of former pupils remained as part of the artistic community in Bushey, many of whom served in different regiments. New Zealand born Harold Septimus Power was an official war artist for the Australian Imperial Forces. Like Lucy Kemp-Welch, he was particularly adept at painting horses in action and he worked on some of his large war canvases in the Meadow Studio in Bushey.

John Sylvester 'Jack' Wheelwright, a former Herkomer student with his older brother Rowland, became a distinguished airship pilot in the Royal Naval Air Service. Already established as a talented designer and inventor – he worked at the famous Silver Studio in Hammersmith, like Lewis Jones of Callowland (see p.82), and Sanderson's Fabrics – he volunteered, aged twenty-nine, at the outbreak of war.

By April 1915 Wheelwright was a Flight Sub-Lieutenant, flying patrols as far apart as the Dardanelles and the North Sea. By 1917 he

Print of Bringing up the Guns (1921) *by Harold Septimus Power.*

was awarded the Distinguished Service Cross (DSC) and was being mentioned in despatches. After the war he was briefly involved in developing barrage balloons, before returning to his work as a wallpaper and fabric designer. He continued to use his inventive skills to design the first automatic screen printer. When war broke out again in 1939, having been an Auxiliary in the inter-war years, he joined the RAF again, eventually becoming a Wing Commander. He continued his work on experimental balloons even after he was discharged due to his age in 1942.

William Henry Bennett of 'High Level', Merry Hill Road, Bushey, served as a 2nd Lieutenant with the Sherwood Foresters. He was killed in action on 11 April 1917, aged forty. He is buried at the St Leger British Cemetery in France and is commemorated on the Bushey Cenotaph and on the memorial plaque in St James's Parish Church, Bushey Heath, and at the Bushey Conservative Club, where he was a member.

Bushey Village *by William Henry Bennett.* (Courtesy of the Bushey Museum and Art Gallery)

Heads of Four Soldiers *by William Sewell.* (Courtesy of the Bushey Museum and Art Gallery)

Private William Sewell of the Bedfordshire Regiment was killed in action on 23 April 1917, also aged forty. He was the husband of Margaret Sewell of 'Chester Cottage', Bushey Heath. Their daughter Phillida born in 1910, became an actress appearing in a number of well-known films (*A Room with a View,* 1985; *Maurice,* 1987) and television dramas, (*Prime Suspect; Inner Circles,* 1995). William is buried at the Arras Memorial in France and, like William Bennett, is commemorated on the Bushey Cenotaph and on the memorial in St Peter's Parish Church.

Some local men went on to become national war heroes. Reginald Warneford achieved fame on 7 June 1915, when he destroyed Zeppelin

LZ 37 by dropping bombs on to it from his single-seater Morane aircraft. He was serving in France with No. 1 Squadron of the Royal Naval Air Service (by 1918, this had been renamed 201 Squadron RAF). The blast from the bombs caused his plane to stall and he had to glide down to land. After making repairs he returned to base nine hours later.

Reginald was awarded the VC and Légion d'honneur. Born in India, his obituary in *Flight Magazine* (20 April 1916) gives his address as Satley, Oxhey Avenue, Oxhey. He returned home to a hero's welcome, but two weeks later he was dead, following a flying accident at the Buc Aerodrome, Paris. He is commemorated on a tablet on the south aisle of St Matthew's Parish Church, Oxhey, and with the street name Warnford Place. He is buried in Brompton Cemetery, where the tablet bears the following inscription:

To the Glory of God and in memory of Flight Sub-Lieut R A J Warneford VC Chavalier Legion D'Honneur RN, who attacked and destroyed a Zeppelin airship June 7th 1915 and was accidentally killed when flying in France June 17th 1915. This tablet was erected by the people of Oxhey.

Christopher Cox had been a farm labourer from Kings Langley before he volunteered to serve as a stretcher bearer in the 7th Bedfordshire Regiment. Wounded on the Somme in July 1916, he was back on the Front Line at Achiet-Le-Grand by September, where he won the VC. In the advance Private Cox went forward over the fire-swept ground to single-handedly rescue four men. After collecting the wounded of his own battalion, he then proceeded to do the same for the wounded of the adjoining battalion. On two subsequent days he performed similar work, with no regard for his own safety. Despite the ensuing fuss, he remained a quiet man, working at the local Ovaltine factory after the war. His Victoria Cross is on display at the Imperial War Museum.

Private Edward Warner, born in St Albans, was a postman in Watford before the War. He served in the 1st Bedfordshire Regiment, winning his VC at Ypres in 1915. *The London Gazette* reported on 29 June:

For most conspicuous bravery near 'Hill 60' on 1st May, 1915. After Trench 46 had been vacated by our troops, consequent on a gas attack, Private Warner entered it single-handed in order to prevent the enemy taking possession. Reinforcements were sent to Private Warner, but could not reach him owing to the gas. He then came back and brought up more men, by which time he was completely exhausted, but the trench was held until the enemy's attack ceased. This very gallant soldier died shortly afterwards from the effects of gas poisoning.

'The Late Private Edward Warner VC', Victoria Cross Heroes, 2nd series, No. 47, Gallaher Ltd cigarette card.

His picture subsequently appeared on cigarette cards celebrating VC recipients issued by the tobacco company Gallaher Ltd of Belfast.

Airmen

The Forces based in the Watford area were not confined to the army. At London Colney, an important airfield came into existence, the home of 56 Squadron of the Royal Flying Corps (RFC). London Colney Airfield, now an ordinary cornfield, was used for training before pilots were pitched into the dogfights over France. It was located between the old Shenley Hospital and the current Harperbury Hospital site, north of Shenley village.

56 Squadron, the first to fly the new Sopwith SE5 fighter planes, arrived on 6 February 1917. Their new CO, Major Richard Graham Blomfield, set out to recruit the best men, a task which even included, for morale purposes, establishing a squadron orchestra. His three initial flight commanders were the already famous Captain Albert Ball MC DSO with two bars, and Captains Ian Henry David Henderson and Ernest Foot. Henderson and Foot were unfortunately injured – Foot in a car accident – on the eve of their planned departure for France. Foot was replaced by Captain Henry 'Duke' Meintjes.

The choice of Ball was crucial because of his ability to attract the best leaders and promising pilots, such as future high scoring 'Aces', Lieutenants Gerald Constable Maxwell, Leonard Barlow, and Arthur

Rhys Davids, who all served under him. Ball later added a VC to his collection of medals. He was referred to by Manfred von Richthofen, the 'Red Baron', as 'by far the best English flying man'. A month after joining the squadron, he lay dead in a field in Annouellin, probably after engine failure had caused his plane to crash, with forty-four kills to his name.

Gerald Maxwell also went on to become highly decorated, receiving the VC, DFC and AFC, and amassing twenty-six kills. Arthur Rhys-Davids DSO, MC and bar, who carried out twenty-seven kills, went missing over Roeselare, Belgium, in pursuit of German aircraft on 27 October 1917. Other highly decorated pilots were Cyril Marconi Crowe, who won the MC and DFC, and the Canadian, Reginald Theodore Carlos Hoidge who won the MC and bar, and had twenty-eight kills. Cecil Arthur Lewis MC, went on to become one of the founders of the BBC and an author. He wrote the wartime novel, *Sagittarius Rising* (1936), which later became part of the inspiration for the 1976 film *Aces High*. Blomfeld worked his pilots hard, but allowed them to enjoy the proximity of London in their free time. After 56 Squadron's last meal together on 6 April 1917 at the Old Red Lion in Radlett, before leaving for Vert Galant the next day, all pilots are said to have returned early and sober.

Once 56 Squadron was in France it was replaced in February 1918 by No. 74 Squadron RAF, known as a 'Tiger Squadron' from its tiger's head motif. It had been formed on 1 July 1917 from a training unit at Northolt flying Avro 504Ks. Edward Corringham 'Mick' Mannock VC DSO MC was appointed flight commander and put in charge of the training programme. The Squadron received its first operational fighters, the SE 5As, before being posted to its base in France at Clairmarais, near St Omer, on 20 March. Mannock died on 26 July 1918, having achieved sixty-one kills.

The Squadron served in France until February 1919, when it returned to Britain. It was disbanded on 3 July 1919. Commanded by a New Zealander, Major Keith Caldwell CBE MC DFC and bar, there were more Americans and Commonwealth pilots in the Squadron as well as the usual Eton and Oxbridge intake.

One pilot, Captain Roderick Leopold Keller MC, from Hadley Wood, Middlesex and a former pupil of Rugby School, is buried in the south-west corner of the graveyard of St Botolph's Church (now a private residence) in Shenleybury. Attached to 41 TD Squadron, he was killed, aged twenty-five, in a flying accident at London Colney on 15 August 1918, whilst flying a Sopwith Snipe (E7998).

Conscription

The policy of conscription was a widely unpopular and controversial measure for the British Government to introduce. At the beginning of 1915 volunteer enlistments ran at about 100,000 a month. Asquith's coalition government had avoided conscription hitherto, but when this figure fell to around 80,000 they were forced to intervene. At first they tried raising the upper age limit from thirty-eight to forty in May, but it was becoming clear that voluntary recruitment alone could not provide the manpower required. A National Registration Act was passed on 15 July to list all available men aged fifteen to sixty-five. These individuals were then to be targeted through advertising and public meetings, the use of propaganda focusing on tales of German atrocities, and the threat of public shame.

As the *Watford Illustrated* reported in August 1915, the census, which it called 'the latest "Doomsday"', would inform the Government of any 'young man of military age, who has not yet done his bit for his country' and he would have to own up to it by putting on his form 'some reason and justification for holding back'.

The results of the census showed there were almost 5 million men of military age not yet in the forces, including 1.6 million in protected occupations, such as those requiring special skills. Asquith appointed Lord Derby, who had opposed conscription, as Director-General of Recruitment. Derby introduced the Group Scheme, commonly known as 'the Derby Scheme', to encourage men to register voluntarily, on the principle that once registered they could defer their service and be transferred into Section B Army Reserve. An added incentive was that married men would only be called up once the supply of single men had been exhausted.

In Watford men queued outside the Recruitment Centre at No. 62 Queen's Road, with those who volunteered before their call up gaining the opportunity of extra training. Despite extensive publicity the Derby Scheme fell short of expectations and was abandoned in December 1915.

Around 500,000 more men were reaching military age each year.

By late September 1915, voluntary enlistment had brought 2.5 million men under arms, but almost two in every five volunteers were entirely unsuitable for military service on the grounds of health. This meant that there was still a shortfall and the government, guided by Lloyd George, was finally resigned to introducing conscription. On 2 March 1916 the Military Service Act came into force. The Act specified that men from eighteen to forty-five years old were liable to be called up for service in the army, unless they were married, widowed with children, serving in the Royal Navy, a minister of religion, or working in one of a number of reserved occupations. A second Act in May 1916 extended liability for military service to married men, and a third Act in 1918 extended the upper age limit to fifty-one. By March 1917, 800 men from Bushey, out of a population of under 8,000, were serving in the forces.

Men could apply to their local military tribunals for various exemptions dependent on circumstances. If declined, they could take their case to the County Appeal Tribunals. There were seven grounds on which exemption could be claimed, including economic grounds (preserving a business), hardship (having a family to support), and ill health or infirmity. Among the sample of records kept in the National Archives, nearly half of the cases were dismissed. Many of the appeals subsequently accepted were granted only a temporary exemption of a few months. The Department of Recruiting at the War Office issued a system of classification: 'A' – men fit for general service; 'B' – men fit for service abroad in a support capacity; 'C' – men fit for service at home only. Each category was additionally graded from one to three, with category three being the weakest.

The results of appeals cases were reported in the local press. The *Watford Observer* of February 1917 reported that G.A.P. Warren, thirty-six, a painter and decorator of Gladstone Road, who had appealed on the grounds of domestic hardship, was passed C2, thus unfit for active service overseas, on the condition that he remained in work of national importance. F. Marland, thirty-three, of Sandringham Road, a munitions worker and the sole support of his invalid father, did not fare so well. After medical examination he was found fit for active service.

Widowed mothers appealed for sons on the grounds that they already had sons who were serving or had been killed, and their youngest was all they had left. The chairman of the tribunal could show some compassion, perhaps deferring call up to a later date. But as the tearful mother of an eighteen-year-old butcher's assistant, with three sons already serving and a fourth dead, put it, 'I hope, please God, the war will be over by then.'

Objectors

Many Christian communities were initially against the idea of a war, but once Germany invaded Belgium there was a widespread change of heart, with even the clergy becoming evangelical about the cause. Anti-war feeling then focused on opposition to universal conscription and afterwards, once that debate was lost, became concerned by the 16,000 conscientious objection was a phenomenon unparalleled in Europe where conscription was already long established. In the first months of conscription there was little sympathy for objectors. Some were sent to France, where they could face a Field General Courts Martial. On 2 July 1916, thirty-four conscientious objectors were sentenced to death, but they had their sentences immediately commuted to ten years' penal servitude.

Applications for exemption were usually made on either religious or political grounds. Those who belonged to faith groups advocating non-violence, such as the Quakers, who had a strong following across the county, could give religious reasons. Others merely rejected what they saw as the jingoism and imperialistic motivations behind a war undertaken for political reasons. Religious objectors were usually dealt with less harshly by the Tribunals. Politically motivated objectors were prevalent in socialist areas, of which there were a number in the region.

The No-Conscription Fellowship, a pacifist organization consisting mainly of Quakers and Independent Labour Party (ILP) supporters, was founded in November 1915. The Fellowship did extensive advocacy work in support of conscientious objectors and produced publications with relevant information. In general, however, public opinion was unsympathetic to those who were, for whatever reason, reluctant to partake in the war effort.

On 15 May 1916 H. Rivers Wilson, a retired Metropolitan Police Inspector living in Letchworth, wrote to the Home Office (his letter is preserved in the National Archives) to complain about the activities of the ILP and the Fellowship in his area. They were holding meetings and in particular distributing 'large quantities of leaflets and pamphlets', one of which, 'Shall Britons be Conscripts', caused Wilson particular offence. Wilson's complaints had already reached the Police Chief in Hatfield but in the meantime, to his dismay, the propaganda was being disseminated, 'with unabated, nay increasing, energy; the net result up to the present being a crop of 32 "Conscientious Objectors", but I suspect that its baleful effects will not be fully felt or understood until the time comes for putting into practice the forthcoming Military Service Act'.

It is estimated that, due to their refusal to fight, at least a third of all conscientious objectors spent some time in prison during the war. Conditions were harsh and many of them suffered physical or mental health problems as a result. The 1,500 'absolutists', those conscientious objectors who took a hard line stance of complete non-involvement in any aspect of the war effort, were locked up for the duration of the conflict. In all, 279 Quakers were imprisoned. Others entered ambulance work (such as The Friends Ambulance Unit) or relief work abroad as an alternative, or accepted non-combatant work on various projects described as of 'national importance'.

After the war, many objectors found it harder than former servicemen to obtain work and in some cases suffered ostracism or even abuse from their fellow-workers. Reflecting the strong Quaker and pacifist sympathies in Hertfordshire, according to the *Watford Observer* in February 1917, there had been 1,200 claims by conscientious objectors in Watford alone: 140 were dismissed; 500 were granted a conditional exemption (i.e. exemption on the condition that they undertook alternative civilian work); and 560 were granted temporary exemption.

From the outset not everyone had been caught up in the euphoria that had accompanied mobilization. The *Watford Illustrated* reported that on the very first Sunday of the War a 'Socialist' meeting held in Watford Market was broken up when members of the large crowd upset the platform, after one of the speakers made 'disrespectful remarks with regard to the King and Lord Kitchener'. The Communist theorist Leon Trotsky, who had predicted the inevitability of the events of the summer, saying that 'History had already poised its gigantic soldier's boot over the anthill,' advocated a socialist anti-war position, and many of his followers, in the spirit of internationalism, did not agree with the concept of fighting their worker comrades.

Anti-war rhetoric had not dimmed by May 1916. Under the title 'A Divine Comedy of Watford', the *Socialist Standard* gave a colourful version of a local Tribunal at which a group of communists and members of the No-Conscription Fellowship from Bushey and Watford appeared. The Tribunal was chaired by Lord Clarendon, with, as they put it, 'the familiar result'. Asked if they were Quakers, the appellants put forward their case as 'Internationalists', Marxists and Atheists.

> *Although Comrade Wilkins explained on his appeal paper that he could more effectively assassinate Rothschild with a new ideal or a new economic law than with an old hatchet ... they still enquired whether he was prepared to take life. He replied that he did not believe in the sacredness of the individual existence, only in the sacredness of humanity, and would therefore help to establish Socialism by the ballot if possible but by force if force was essential.*

In the end the cases were dismissed and the defendants were allowed to appeal to the County Tribunal. Then:

> *the "Red Flag" was sung, and just as it ended the Constable entered the room and faced the perplexed Tribunal and those pigment Councillors on the walls, whose pensive eyes are fixed on the distant Utopian Watford when each of the ten thousand inhabitants was docile and diligent and none had dreamed of Marxian Economics.*

In contrast, Ronald Morley Hooper, a confirmed pacifist with socialist sympathies, had joined up in late 1915. He resisted the first call to arms, but increasingly felt that as a single man he was not 'doing his bit'. The son of a Nonconformist minister, he was a master at the Royal Masonic School in Bushey, where most of the other teachers who were fit for service had already left to fight. Once at the Front he slowly moved away from his pacifism and transferred from being an Observer to the Royal Engineers, hoping to be closer to the action. Ronald was killed in an explosion in France on 18 March 1918, the opening day of the Spring Offensive, Germany's last attempt to win the war through a decisive action.

CHAPTER 2

Civilian Life

The Great War was a total war fought as much on the Home Front as in the Trenches. Within months it became clear that to win the War the endeavours of the whole nation would have to be channelled into the war effort.

In March 1915 the poor quality of the shells provided to the army led to a crisis which brought down Asquith's Liberal government. The 'shell scandal' enabled the formation of a coalition between the Liberals and the Conservatives, with Asquith still as Prime Minister and Lloyd George, a Liberal, as Minister of Munitions. The more bullish Lloyd George put the national economy on a war footing and subsequently the supply of ammunition improved.

In the meantime advances in technology had brought the British civilian population into the Front Line for the first time in centuries. In December 1914, the North East coastal towns of West Hartlepool, Scarborough and Whitby were shelled by the German Navy, causing a 'serious loss of life' (*Hartlepool Gazette*). In the South East of England, air raids became a reality and the guns of Flanders could even be heard as far away as Bushey, a constant reminder of the conflict.

For the population of south-west Hertfordshire the immediate consequences of going to war were varied. Prominent local dignitaries sprang into action with the same vigour as those mobilizing the troops; Lady Essex led the way in organizing volunteers and fund-raising. Lower down the social scale, in the first week many factories closed and some workers were put on shorter hours. There was a spate of panic buying. People with cars loaded them up with foodstuffs and the shops were stripped to such an extent that some stores closed early, the demand causing a rise in prices.

Instances of stockpiling continued throughout the war. As late as 1918, when fears of invasion had not completely disappeared, a resident of Common Wood House in Chipperfield was accused of hoarding large quantities of tea, sugar, bacon, rice, oatmeal, Quaker oats, jam, and other assorted foodstuffs. For this the defendant was fined £350 plus costs and 90 per cent of the food was confiscated.

DEFENCE OF THE REALM. E.P. 6.

MINISTRY OF FOOD.

BREACHES OF THE RATIONING ORDER

The undermentioned convictions have been recently obtained:—

Court	Date	Nature of Offence	Result
HENDON - -	29th Aug., 1918	Unlawfully obtaining and using ration books -	3 Months' Imprisonment
WEST HAM -	29th Aug., 1918	Being a retailer & failing to detach proper number of coupons	Fined £20
SMETHWICK -	22nd July, 1918	Obtaining meat in excess quantities - - -	Fined £50 & £5 5s. costs
OLD STREET -	4th Sept., 1918	Being a retailer selling to unregistered customer	Fined £72 & £5 5s. costs
OLD STREET -	4th Sept., 1918	Not detaching sufficient coupons for meat sold -	Fined £25 & £2 2s. costs
CHESTER-LE-STREET	4th Sept., 1918	Being a retailer returning number of registered customers in excess of counterfoils deposited - - - -	Fined £50 & £5 5s. costs
HIGH WYCOMBE	7th Sept., 1918	Making false statement on application for and using Ration Books unlawfully - - - - - - - -	Fined £40 & £6 4s. costs

Enforcement Branch, Local Authorities Division.
MINISTRY OF FOOD.
September 1918

Breaches of Rationing Poster outlining common rationing offences, September 1918.

War brought uncertainty to the commercial sector, with disruption to imports and exports and fear of a decline in home trade. In the first week, Blyth & Platt's Cobra Works in Bushey announced: 'trade seriously affected by the war'. The manufacture of boot polish depended on imported raw materials and their market was largely based on exports. In consequence their business suffered and they were forced to put their workers, many of whom were women, on half-time. The printers André & Sleigh had their private orders cancelled and their exports also ceased (their fortunes improved subsequently). At the same time Emily Beale, 'Corset Expert' of Queen's Road, felt the need to place adverts in the *Watford Observer* exhorting all ladies to support the war effort by buying British.

There were also opportunities for some businesses. Benskins Brewery secured a lucrative export market supplying beer to Belgium via canal to the London docks, presumably for the British Army. They continued to expand their activities, taking over a further two small breweries in Bishop's Stortford and Aston, Buckinghamshire, in 1915.

Every aspect of people's lives would soon be affected, from the nature of their work to the extent of their freedoms. The government found it increasingly necessary to interfere, either by taking control of the railways and key industries or by curtailing civil liberties and manipulating public will through the unprecedented use of propaganda. Some changes were for the good, if for example your wages improved due to better paid war work, but on the whole the population would be required to make sacrifices.

For many the profound nature of these sacrifices and the reasons behind them needed further explanation. The records of Beechen Grove Baptist Church, Watford, note that the Anniversary Service held in September 1914 was 'heavy with the gloom of war'. The tenor of the service was one in which the conflict was seen as a spiritual struggle, the message being that the German anti-Christian philosopher Friedrich Nietzsche (1844–1900) was to be held responsible for Germany's militarism.

Similarly, in January 1915, Kate Murphy BA gave ten in-depth lectures on the 'History and Literature relating to the War' in Watford Public Library, with the first session chaired by Lord Clarendon. The talks were by no means light, adopting a wide-ranging and intellectual tone. Topics included: the history of Germany, with attention to the rise of Prussia and 'the Teuton and the Slav'; German writers such as Goethe, Nietzsche (and his philosophy of the Superman) and Heinrich von Treitsche, a German nationalist historian and eulogist of the house of Hohenzollern, whose latest incumbent was Kaiser Wilhelm II, the German Emperor. Murphy also covered Austria and Hungary; contemporary France, with talks on the novelists Anatole France and Romain Rolland; and the Franco-German War; Russia and her relations to the Slavic Nations and the novelists, Tolstoy and Dostoyevsky; and finally Belgium and the nineteenth century diplomat Klemens von Metternich, who had tried to maintain the ideal of a balance of power within Europe.

Freedom of speech, however, could no longer be taken for granted. On 8 August 1914, only four days into the War, the Defence of the Realm Act (DORA) was passed. Though initially only a paragraph long (it was revised and expanded over the following years) it immediately gave the government wide-ranging additional powers. For instance, private buildings, land or materials needed for the war effort could now be requisitioned and laws were tightened up. In rural areas this meant farmers lost carts and wagons to the military. Anti-war activists could be sent to prison and trial by courts martial was authorized for individuals contravening regulations designed 'to prevent the spread of false reports or reports likely to cause disaffection to His Majesty'.

Censorship was introduced, with the consequence that news stories 'not in the national interest' could result in prosecution, and the discussion of naval and military activities was limited as much as possible. Previously innocent activities, such as flying kites, starting bonfires, buying binoculars, feeding wild animals bread or buying alcohol on public transport, became proscribed. Alcoholic beverages were watered down and early closing for pubs was introduced, with opening times restricted to noon to 3.00pm and 6.30pm to 9.30pm. To the displeasure of farmers and industrial workers, in order to maximize productivity, Daylight Saving was introduced in May 1916, in the form of British Summer Time.

Income tax rose considerably, the standard rate growing from 6 per cent in 1914 to 30 per cent in 1918, while the number of taxpayers also increased from 1.13 million to 3 million. The call up of able-bodied men for active service had an impact across the spectrum of employment, causing labour shortages, not only in industry and agriculture, but in shops, schools, local health care services and government. Very early on it was recognised that economies would have to be made. By 1915 the Watford Gas and Coke Co. was running adverts in the *Watford Observer* claiming that cooking and heating by gas was 'A great saving for wartime', as it could be turned off by tap like water, and The World Stores advertised themselves as 'Pioneers in Popular Prices' and leaders in 'Food Economy'. As shortages increased rationing became inevitable, with a variety of results, from non-urgent works being put on hold and hospital meals reduced for patients and staff.

The First Christmas

On 9 January 1915, the *Watford Observer* published a letter by Signaller Percival (Percy) Edward Tarver, a Bushey resident enlisted as a Private with the London Territorials and serving in Neuve-Chapelle in France. He described the famous 1914 Christmas Truce:

> *the Germans began Christmassing on the 24th, and actually waved little illuminated Christmas trees, and stopped firing ... I don't know actually when or how the truce began but some say a few Germans came out unarmed and shouted: 'Don't shoot for two days and we won't'. Anyway, on Christmas morning both sides came out, and met and 'swopped' cigarettes. Lots of them spoke English ... They even talked of arranging a football match.*

Sadly Percy was killed not long after the truce, on 2 March 1915, aged forty-two.

It was also reported that the English offered the Germans Christmas pudding in exchange for German black bread. Every serving man from Abbots Langley received a gift of plum pudding, chocolate, tobacco and cigarettes and a Christmas card, donated by all the residents of the village; a gift they continued until 1917.

In contrast to the feel-good stories from the Front, Lance Sergeant Thomas Edward Gregory, of the Hertfordshire Regiment, from St James Road in Watford was shot in Lille on Christmas Day. Thomas had been attempting to take out a sniper who had killed his comrade Private Percy Higgins from Ware. His wife Jeanette did not receive the news until January. She had just given birth to their seventh child, who was named Lille, after the place where her father died. Thomas had been a postman before the war and the difficulties of Jeanette's new life as a single mother with a large family were eased somewhat with help from the Post Office. The company looked after the children, sending the boys off to boarding school and the two younger girls to Watford Grammar School for Girls.

At home the progress of the war, reported with an upbeat spin, was taking up more space in the local press. The *Watford Observer* noted that at home the conflict had brought a truce to the political struggle. Christmas was being held as normally as possible, with the customary Church festivities and Christmas trees in the shops, but the Forces were not forgotten. Donated Christmas puddings not only found their way out to Percy Tarver's trench, but were also sent to the Fleet.

For the troops still in Britain, special seasonal activities were laid on. In Watford a Christmas Dinner was given to Major Colette and seventy-seven men of the King Edward's Horse, in St John's Hall. Afterwards J. H. Clements, on behalf of the committee responsible, gave thanks to the many donors. For the wives and children of the men serving, entertainment was provided by the War Wives and Mothers Association in Oxhey Parish Hall and on New Year's Eve, the Bushey Soldiers and Sailors Families Association gave a tea to the wives and children in the Parish Hall.

Shortages

The combination of a poor American wheat harvest in 1916 and heavy losses of merchant shipping due to German U-boat activity led to a shortage of flour and some other food supplies. In January 1917, the boys of the Royal Masonic School in Bushey were restricted to two slices of bread and margarine for their tea, and white bread was banned altogether. On 23 April, Hertfordshire County Council sent out a Shortage of Bread Notice to headteachers, in an attempt to put pressure on families.

Schoolchildren were often used as a conduit to influence their parents. The Bread Notice suggested that if you ate 2½lbs of meat then you were entitled to 4lbs of bread per week, but the more meat you ate the less bread you were allowed, as meat was then still relatively plentiful. Gardening was introduced on to the school curriculum and schools contributed to local food production by turning school fields into vegetable patches. Merry Hill and Ashfield Boys, Bushey, grew potatoes on theirs.

Ration books were issued in 1918. Although sugar was almost unobtainable from the beginning of the War, it only went on ration from 1 January 1918. People could apply for additional amounts for jam making, provided that they owned the fruit. The rationing of meat and butter followed. Meat was rationed by a third per head per week and coupons were exchanged for cash. Throughout the county long queues began to form outside shops and head teachers complained that parents were using their children to hold places in the queue for them. Prices were pushed up and there were particular shortages in tea, sugar, butter, margarine and potatoes. In Hemel Hempstead things got so bad that emergency supplies had to be delivered and Kings Langley acquired a reputation as the 'Hungry Village'. Jack Scott, who worked in the paper mills, recalled that, with ingenuity, there were ways to supplement your diet such as catching rabbits on the Common.

By 1915 the effects of shortage of labour on the land were being felt and the Government deemed it necessary to encourage women to become involved in food production. The Board of Trade began sending agricultural organizing officers around the country in an effort to persuade resistant farmers to accept women workers. The Women's Land Army was finally introduced in 1917 and these exhortations resulted in over 260,000 women working as farm labourers with 20,000 in the Land Army itself.

Women were involved in all aspects of agricultural work, to the disapproval of some traditionalists. The wearing of trousers and the liberated behaviour of women out and about on their own in public was frowned upon, but with time it was realized that increased visibility was not necessarily synonymous with loose morals. Their wages and conditions were set by the Agricultural Wages Board. The agreed wage for someone over the age of 18 was £1 12 pence a week, after deductions had been made for lodgings and food, working a maximum of 50 hours in the summer and 48 hours in the winter, with Saturday afternoons and Sundays off. These conditions were not always met and there were reports of exploitation.

On 4 March 1916 the *Hemel Hempstead Gazette* reported that Hertfordshire County Council had set up its own register for 'organising women's labour on the land'. It went on to announce the following October that:

> *The neighbouring farmers have been very pleased with the way the women* [of Leaverstock Green] *have helped them on the land. About 24 have enrolled since Easter ... 27 women have earned the green armlet which is given for 30 days work on the farm, and can be obtained through the District Secretaries of the Herts Woman's War Agricultural Council. This is a good record for women, by far the greater number of whom have never worked in the field before.*

Enlistment in the Land Army meant that women could be posted to varied locations. Emma Jolly, from Streatham in London was trained in Highcroft in Hertfordshire and then worked on the Arkley Rise estate near Barnet feeding hens, milking cows and churning butter. The seventeen-year-old Florence Fremantle, from Swanbourne in Buckinghamshire, whose brother Halford had died in the trenches in 1915, enlisted in the Land Army to serve the war effort and honour Halford's memory. The daughter of Lord Cottesloe, Colonel of the Bucks Battalion Territorial Army, she was a talented artist. At Brockhold Farm near Ware she sketched and wrote poems, including a song to encourage national recruitment. After the War Florence became a missionary in Palestine and Egypt, and later worked for the BBC's Arabic News Service.

Despite 2,000 women being involved in fieldwork in the county, 500 soldiers were still needed to assist in gathering in the harvest. As the land already under cultivation soon proved insufficient, local authorities had the power to requisition land for temporary allotments. The *Watford Observer* of 2 February 1918 noted that '87 acres of permanent allotments and 64 acres of National allotments allocated and still trying for more.' The sports pitches of King George's Recreation Ground, Bushey (founded 1912) were turned into allotments, with six acres given to the cultivation of potatoes. Despite the difficulties, there were few cases of real hardship and in many instances families were better nourished than before the War. Local death rates fell during the period too, as food was more fairly distributed between rich and poor.

Morale

For a few weeks at the outset of the conflict all churches experienced a surge in participation, as people sought comfort and guidance. There was an identification with the justness of Britain's cause and a fusing of religion with patriotism. Large numbers of churchgoers volunteered for the armed forces, changing the demographic of the congregations, which were now disproportionately made up of women.

As the conflict took its toll, however, and the military casualties and domestic sacrifices mounted, regular attendance by Protestants fell away. Church attendance was particularly affected within the Nonconformist tradition, which was well represented in Hertfordshire.

Roman Catholic attendance seems to have held up, perhaps in part due to the large presence of Belgian refugees. The public became disillusioned with the Church, feeling that Church leaders had not done enough to prevent or shorten the War. Some people found alternative forms of spiritual expression, particularly in Spiritualism.

As the War dragged on, the hardships of the Home Front – augmented by the slow war of attrition on the battlefield and news of a revolution in Russia – had serious consequences for public morale. In response to this and to unrest amongst workers, in 1917 Lloyd George set up a cross-party National War Aims Committee to act as a propaganda tool. Local areas had their own committees, which were allowed an element of autonomy in selecting their own speakers. In Watford the organizers, reflecting the mood of the time, asked for the Trades Unionists and Labour politicians, the Minister of Food, J.R. Clynes or the anti-conscriptionist, J.H. Thomas, but autonomy only went so far and they had to settle for another Trades Unionist Labour MP, Charles Duncan.

Those on the Left had an uneasy relationship with the war effort. In February 1918, Councillor Fred H. Gorle gave an address to the Labour Church in Durban Road, Watford on 'The Bolshevik Peril to British Labour'. The Labour Church was something of an anachronism, especially in the South of England. A Christian Socialist movement, it had been in decline for several years and was virtually extinct by the beginning of the War. Gorle was a prominent member of the movement and a former President.

The Watford branch, which featured decorations by the Art Nouveau designer Walter Crane and the slogan 'Workers of the World Unite' above the podium, was originally founded in 1900 and had connections with the British Socialist Party of London (Watford). It could attract speakers as prominent as the Labour leader and pacifist Keir Hardie. Nevertheless, the upheaval of the War finally brought the Church to an end. This general shift in politics to the left was reflected in the formation of a branch of the Labour Party in Bushey in April 1918.

Requisitioning

During the first autumn of the war, 100,000 billets were acquired across Hertfordshire for troops in training. By early 1915 at least 250,000 men, often many more, were stationed in Watford, Berkhamsted, St Albans and Bishop's Stortford. These men could be billeted in the centre of town. For instance, the 54th East Anglian Division were in Queens Road, Watford, at the end of May 1915, before leaving for Gallipoli. They had arrived together with the Norfolk Regiment who departed in July.

Soon the region was so brimming with army personnel that officers and policemen toured the outlying districts, searching for additional accommodation and the neighbouring villages did not escape. Houses were marked 'ASC' (Army Service Corps) with the number of people to be billeted added. Initially the soldiers were received enthusiastically, being cheered, offered sweets and cigarettes and welcomed into homes. Gradually the constant billeting and change of occupants took its toll, unsettling families. Although there was a billeting allowance to offset costs, this did not include meals, which families were not required to provide. Consequently many poorer families found it hard to maintain their initial burst of hospitality.

The Inns of Court OTC (Officer Training Corps), nicknamed 'The Devil's Own', were billeted in Berkhamsted in September 1914. The next May, Francis Buckley found himself lodged with Mr. Charles Dipple from 'whose family' he recalled he 'received much kind hospitality'. The hard work and changed surroundings were a shock to the system he felt, 'a sudden change for one who had spent the greater part of ten years in London chambers'.

Men were billeted throughout the town, with some also sleeping under canvas. Oliver Pearson wrote home to his family in Nottinghamshire to say that he 'was extremely lucky' to be given a bed at 24 Victoria Road 'as most were billeted in sheds in a wood-yard'. over 12,000 troops passed through the training camp, leaving 13,000 yards of trenches on the Common. The impact on a town with a population of only 7,500 was huge. By 1916 the residents had begun to feel the strain, airing their grievances in the local press, with the issue of billeted soldiers becoming deeply divisive.

Public and private buildings were turned over to war purposes, many local councils giving up their properties willingly. In 1914 a company of the Post Office Rifles was billeted for a few months in the Recreation Hall of Leavesden Asylum; the officers were quartered with the Medical Superintendent. The company was part of the 47th (1/2nd

London) Division, one of the first-line Territorial divisions mobilized for full-time war service on 5 August 1914 and based around the St Albans area by mid-August. The division stayed for around seven months before leaving for Southampton. They arrived in France on 18 March 1915, where they then served for the duration of the War.

As they were about to depart from Leavesden, one rifleman wrote home:

> *There was a final inspection: all on leave recalled: felt sorry for them. Rumours wild about imminent embarkation. Will be sorry to say good-bye to the inmates of Leavesden Lunatic Asylum, where our company has been billeted for the past few months. We got to know and much to like the inmates and their peculiar ways. Some very factual and sensible to the degree of telling us we were the barmy ones going to war never to return.*

The hospital did not only provide beds. In response to the need for more farmland and the Board of Agriculture's directive that more pastureland should be made available for the breeding of livestock, the football field was fenced off and the hospital's farmland leased out. Space in what would perhaps be thought of as an unusual public amenity became available with the decline in the national prison population, which had begun at the turn of the century and accelerated during the War. The number of convicted prisoners fell from 136,000 in 1913-14 to 43,000 in 1916-17, with the result locally that St Albans Prison was handed over to the Home Office in 1916.

Schools could be taken over at a moment's notice. During the summer holiday of 1914 troops occupied ten schools in St Albans and, despite protests from parents, as the beginning of term approached, they showed no sign of leaving. Eventually room was made in nearby large private houses for dislodged classes from the prestigious High School, but the elementary schools received few offers of help. A month after the beginning of term it was decided to cram the elementary school children into five partly vacated schools. The homeless Priory Park School was squeezed in together with the Hatfield Road School, with disastrous results, as each class was forced to double up. During the summer of 1915 the school briefly returned to its normal premises, only for the exercise to be repeated the following winter.

Hemel Hempstead Education Committee took a tougher line. In August 1914 the army commandeered all public and many private buildings, including re-opening the town's public baths, which had been closed for over twenty years, to provide facilities for the troops. They evicted the town's schoolchildren into totally inadequate facilities, threatening to bring all education provision to a standstill. After futile protests the Committee took a delegation to the War Office and Board of Education, securing the reluctant evacuation of four schools. With the use of Sunday Schools and Congregational, Baptist and Salem chapels for the overflow, the school term began on time.

In November 1914, 130 soldiers were billeted in Beechen Grove Baptist Church School House, in Red Lion Yard (now demolished) in Watford; an action that may have led to the disbanding of the local Boys' Brigade, which folded at this time. The Baptists at Leavesden Green also had their Chapel used as a billet. Nor did the Anglicans of St Andrews escape; their church hall was requisitioned in 1914.

When the army required the use of four elementary schools in Watford in October 1915, lessons had been learnt and a shift system was introduced. Four schools not required by the army became the hosts for two shifts of children from eight schools, sharing the premises on a rota. The playground of Parkgate School in Watford was turned into a kitchen for the troops. In January 1916 three more schools were handed over to the army and the shift system was extended to include these and two more host schools. Thirteen of the twenty-three schools were disrupted, involving 3,184 children. The army spent the summer under canvas but returned at the end of the year. With the disruption to the buildings and the lives of children and staff, it was natural for the continued presence of the troops to cause resentment; despite this, those affected made the best of the situation.

Sometimes the army found more appropriate or conducive surroundings. The Woodside Retreat fairground attraction in the woods of Brikett Wood was taken over as a camp. After the war it was re-opened but never regained its former success, closing for good in 1929. A number of private buildings were lent or acquired too. In the grounds of Hatfield House, the Jacobean home of the Marquise of Salisbury, the devastation of no-man's land was recreated, complete with trenches, craters and barbed-wire, in order to test the new Mark 1 tank.

A little lower down the scale, Bushey Hall, which had become a high-class country hotel at the beginning of the century, was used for officer training by the Household Brigade during the last part of the war. One of their number, Eustace George St Clair Chance died, aged nineteen, on 27 September 1918 and is remembered on the Trinity College War Memorial, Cambridge. He had joined the 2nd Coldstream Guards at Windsor, after leaving Eton in December 1917, becoming a 2nd Lieutenant. He is buried at Sanders Keep Military Cemetery, Graincourt-Les-Havrincourt, France. Many of his fellow officer cadets who survived the Great War went on to become distinguished commanders in World War Two.

Lululand, Sir Hubert von Herkomer's fantasy home in Bushey, nicknamed the 'Bavarian Castle', was briefly requisitioned but never put to military use. Towards the end of the war, the Queen Mary's Auxiliary Army Corps was billeted in Bushey and some members stayed there. Formed in 1917 as the Women's Army Auxiliary Corps (WAAC) and renamed in 1918, it was essentially a civilian formation, the women being initially deployed in France as cooks and waitresses.

After Herkomer's death in March 1914, Lady Herkomer had moved out. His son Siegfried enlisted in May 1915, after the sinking of the *Lusitania*, in which two American art students from the School and a Miss Clay from Bushey died. As a result of Herkomer's interest in film-making, part of the building was used from 1913 by the Bushey Film Corporation. In 1915 the studios in Melbourne Road were acquired by The British Actors Film Company, a consortium of prominent stage actors that included A.E. Mathews and Leslie Howard.

Mathews lived locally in Little Bushey Lane and Howard had been invalided out of the Northamptonshire Yeomanry in 1916 with shell shock. Howard, who spent time in Bushey, was involved through his uncle Wilfred Noy, a director at the studio. The company produced a number of silent dramas and made itself available for propaganda purposes, although there is little evidence of this being taken up. It also claimed to provide work for discharged soldiers. Never a robust concern, it succumbed to financial difficulties in 1923. Lululand meanwhile fell derelict. It subsequently remained largely unoccupied and, due to increasing expense, was almost completely demolished in 1939, with only a remnant of the façade, the front door and its tympanum, surviving to become the frontage of a Royal British Legion Club until 2012.

Even after the War was over some buildings were still required by the army. In May 1919 the *Watford Observer* reported that the military wanted to retain North End House, Clarendon Hall, the Skating Rink, Beechen Grove School House and Halsley Masonic Hall. Little Nascot and Chater School were to be vacated.

Air Raids

The novelty of war in the air brought British civilians right into the firing line, and the fear of air raids became a reality, even in remote areas. For instance, the flight path of the Zeppelin airships heading for north London took them over central Hertfordshire. Germany's bombing campaign began in January 1915. The raids took place by night and in their early stages they proved haphazard and inaccurate; one raid on the capital succeeding in bombing Hull instead. From 1917 onwards, when night raids were supplemented by daylight bombing, heavily armed Gotha G-V bomber aircraft were brought in to replace the Zeppelins, which had proved to be increasingly vulnerable.

In response searchlights, anti-aircraft guns and aircraft were deployed. London was defended by a number of searchlight and gun batteries stretching across its northern approaches and into Hertfordshire, which were reinforced as the attacks intensified. Units were in place as far as Hemel Hempstead, and in the surrounding villages of Gadebridge, Boxmoor, Bovingdon and Flaunden.

German bombs were not the only problem. In 1917 the Royal Masonic School for Girls in Rickmansworth was damaged by anti-aircraft fire. Other less potentially destructive precautions could be taken. In 1916 the tall chimney of the recently closed Brickfields brick and tile works near Elstree and Borehamwood Station was demolished, for fear it would attract enemy attention.

The unnerving lights, the sound of aircraft, guns and explosions during an air raid could be experienced for miles around. One unexpected result of the raids on London was the influx of people anxious to escape the bombings, who moved into the neighbourhood of Oxhey or bought up houses in Watford, evicting the tenants, who were often soldiers' wives with young families. By 1918 the increase in population in Chorleywood, as a result of the evacuation of children and the billeting of soldiers, was causing a major crisis to the village's sewage system.

No official government blackout was imposed in response to the air raids, matters being largely dealt with at a local level. At a council meeting in Chorleywood in June 1915 it was decided to restrict lighting, and the police in Bushey similarly suggested dimming the streetlights, while in Watford on twenty-three occasions all lights were extinguished in the darkened streets because of possible raids. This inevitably had a knock-on effect, causing shops to cut down their hours. Residents were advised to have mattresses, rugs and hot water bottles at the ready and to lie down by the dividing wall in their house during an air raid. They were also told to avoid putting themselves in danger by watching the action. In Park Street village, the lucky Stanley Giddins, owner of the Park Street Mill, was able to use the cellar of the mill house, normally reserved for beers, wines and spirits, as a shelter. This unfortunately may have contributed to the alcoholism that reportedly led to him having to sell the mill after the War.

The minutes for autumn 1917, written up by the Deacon of Beechen Grove Baptist Church, Watford, record that:

> *At this juncture, an air raid being in progress and the lights lowered, Messrs. Michael and Tait as special constables retired, but before doing so Mr. Michael asked that the advisability of commencing the Sunday evening services at 6pm should be considered.*

As a general response, church windows were darkened and church bells were not rung after dusk. School windows were also blacked out. At Abbots Hill School, south of Hemel Hempstead, the electric lights were 'so swathed in greenery owing to the possible visits of hostile aircraft that they only gave out a faint light akin to that of the moon'. Meanwhile, Ashfield School, Bushey, brought forward afternoon school by half an hour.

Although the bombings appeared fairly random, causing relatively few casualties, people's fears were not unjustified. Cheshunt was raided in September 1915, with little damage, but in October, when a raid destroyed numerous houses in Hertford nine people were killed. The lack of co-ordinated warnings and blackout enforcement meant that a number of the casualties had come out of their houses to watch the airships.

On 3 September 1916, during the largest raid of the war, involving sixteen airships heading for various targets including London, one of the Shutte-Lanz airships, SL-11, passed over St Albans, dropping bombs on London Colney, Hadley Wood and the northern suburbs of London. Turning north over Tottenham and Enfield, it was picked up by searchlights at Waltham Abbey and spotted by Second Lieutenant William Leefe Robinson, of the 39th Home Guard Squadron, who was flying from the airfield known as Sutton's Farm, Hornchurch, in his BE2c biplane. Robinson pursued and engaged the SL-11 and eventually, on his Lewis gun's third drum of ammunition, he succeeded in setting it alight.

Recruitment poster using fear of air raids. (Publicity Department, Central Recruiting Depot, 1915)

The engagement was seen for miles around, and the searchlights and explosions illuminating the night sky were visible as far away as Aylesbury. The SL-11 crashed in a field at Cuffley. A nearby Zeppelin, the L-16 commanded by Erich Sommerfeld, in order to avoid the glow from the SL-11 and the attentions of other planes involved in the chase, headed off to the north. To speed its escape L-16 jettisoned its bomb load over Essendon, about halfway between Hatfield and Hertford, causing considerable damage to the Church of St Mary the Virgin and other buildings nearby. In one of these houses, two daughters of the village blacksmith, Frances and Eleanor Bamford, aged 26 and 12 respectively, were mortally wounded. Meanwhile, the L-32, which had been following behind, decided to turn back, scaring the sheep in Little Gaddesden and dropping bombs over Berkhamsted, Markyate and near Ware.

Commander Wilhelm Schramm and the fifteen-man crew of the SL-11 received a military funeral two days later at Potters Bar Cemetery. Visitors flocked from the surrounding area and parts of the wreckage were sold off by the Red Cross to raise money for wounded soldiers. This was the first time a German airship had been shot down on English soil and Lieutenant Robinson was awarded the VC.

A few weeks later, on 1 October, during a major raid of eleven airships on London, Second Lieutenant Wulstan Joseph Tempest, also of the 39th, scored another success over Potters Bar – one of four Zeppelins brought down in a month. When the L-31 was picked up by the searchlight batteries its commander, Kapitanleutnant Heinrich Mathy, decided to abandon his raid, dropping most of his bombs to lighten the ship. As a result thirty high-explosive and twenty-six incendiary bombs were dropped on Cheshunt, damaging more than 300 houses and destroying six acres of greenhouses, but amazingly only injuring one woman.

Caught in the beams from the Potters Bar and Barnet Searchlight Detachments, Tempest arrived flying in a Bleirot experimental biplane, as Mathy tried to gain height to escape the ant-aircraft fire. In order to avoid being hit himself, Tempest dropped three flares, the signal to the ground batteries to cease firing. He then went in to attack, eventually nailing his target with his incendiary ammunition. Tempest received the DSO for his actions. The nearby L-24, seeing the dramatic fate of its sister ship changed course and dropped all its bombs over Willian aerodrome near Hitchin, perhaps mistaking the runway flares for buildings. There was one fatality: Private William Hawkes of the Royal Defence Corps.

Thousands of spectators watched for miles around as the Zeppelin fell from the sky in a ball of flame caught in the searchlights. Local special constables were kept busy trying to curtail the excitement and enforce the blackout. *The Hemel Hempstead Gazette* reported that the streets were thronged with curious people who had been roused by the noise overhead and the lights in the sky. Their vigil was rewarded by the sight of the distant airship crashing to the ground in flames. Mathy decided to jump rather than burn in the blazing wreckage. Michael MacDonagh, a journalist, saw the 'appalling spectacle' as he crossed Blackfriars Bridge on his way home from his London office. The next day he took a packed train to Potters Bar to see the body of Mathy, 'the most renowned of the German airship commanders', and the indentation his body left in the ground.

Mathy and his eighteen-man crew were buried near to their comrades of the SL-11 in one casket. The bodies of the SL-11 and the L-31 crews were later re-interred at the large military cemetery for the German dead of two World Wars at Cannock Chase, near Birmingham, which was dedicated in 1967.

Initial air raid warnings were amateurish, involving policemen carrying signs on bicycles or Boy Scouts blowing bugles from cars. In Bushey, an air raid was signalled by a car driving up from London from which one of the passengers would ring a bell and shout, "Take cover". In June 1917, the first official air raid warning siren was sounded from a factory in St Albans, but the system proved inefficient, with lack of reliable intelligence creating false alarms and the inexperienced operators also often forgetting to sound the all clear.

Transport in Wartime

The rural roads of Hertfordshire, many of them narrow and winding, were ill equipped for the sudden influx of motorised vehicles and modern military machines on the outbreak of war. In the chaos of villages inundated with unprecedented activity, accidents ensued involving unwary children and pedestrians. As time passed, horse-drawn vehicles slowly gave way to motorised ones, even for general and agricultural use.

In some cases, the solution could be as disruptive as the problem. In 1914, Bushey, despite being on the main London to Watford artery, was said by the County Highways Department to have the worst roads in the county. It was decided to pave the road with wooden blocks, because the labour and materials could be provided locally, yet this merely caused months of disruption. By 1916 the Kilburn to Watford bus route was still on diversion and heavy rain and increased traffic had turned the back roads into mud, making them hazardous for pedestrians.

Once war was declared, Britain's railways were put under Government control and the military had priority, which made journeys to London more difficult. Improvements to the London and North Western Railway (L&NWR), which ran from Euston, had begun before the War. The electrification of the line meant that the Bakerloo Line, run by the Underground Electric Railways Company of London Ltd (UERL), could be extended north from Paddington to Watford Junction via Queens Park, where the lines merged. The work was continued between 1915 and 1917, until the line reached Watford. The resulting expansion intensified the need to employ female workers. The transport historian Christian Wolmar has stated that, 'when the Watford extension of the Bakerloo line opened in 1917, all staff except drivers were women'. Shortage of materials and labour and problems with the rolling stock caused delays, however, and the line remained a weekday only service until 1919.

The outbreak of war also postponed the projected extension of the Metropolitan Line to a proposed terminus in Watford town centre. The present Moon Under Water pub in the High Street was to have been the booking hall for Watford Central Station. By the time work was recommenced in 1922, new financial considerations and a change of heart by the Urban Council meant that when the Watford terminus was completed in 1925 it was situated less conveniently, at the edge of Cassiobury Park.

Despite the war, UERL, the parent company behind the Metropolitan and Bakerloo Lines, was still promoting the leafy attractions of south-west Hertfordshire in 1915. The renowned American artist Edward McKnight Kauffer, who had moved from Paris to London when the war began, produced attractive posters of Oxhey and Watford for the company. They were printed by Waterlow and Sons at their works in Watford.

Edward McKnight Kauffer, Oxhey Woods, *1915* (© TfL from the London Transport Museum collection)

Edward McKnight Kauffer, In Watford, *1915* (© TfL from the London Transport Museum collection)

The railways were also the first local bus operators, as they needed to be able to get passengers to their stations. The L&NWR ran buses from Watford Junction to Croxley Green, Cassiobury, Boxmoor, Garston and Bushey Arches. In April 1915, the L&NWR had to suspend their bus service in the town, due to the number of drivers and conductors joining the Colours. In August 1916, the railway company was petitioned for more stopping trains passing through Callow Land Halt on the Watford–St Albans line to compensate for the lack of bus transport. This was an important stop because of the nearby munitions works.

Business and Employment

The First World War created new working opportunities for women: some in paid employment and others in voluntary roles. One such was to work as auxiliaries to the British Army, something eagerly taken on during 1916 by a Mrs Pilling who was teaching potential cooks for the Army Catering Corps in her kitchen in 'Inveresk', Hempstead Road, Watford. This was an important service, as army units had to take responsibility for sourcing and supplying their own meals. By July 1917, prejudices as to the suitability of women taking a more active role in the army were overcome and an official Women's Army Auxiliary Corps was formed. Women were then sent to the Front to work in units that performed cookery, mechanical, clerical and other miscellaneous supporting tasks.

The draining of male workers from the labour force and their consequent replacement with women had a knock-on effect on Britain's social structure. Women had always worked, but within well-defined boundaries. Most of what was previously regarded as 'women's work' had been in domestic service, and at this time about 12 per cent of the female population of England and Wales were employed as domestic servants. Before the war, the Watford area was well-endowed with great country mansions, large town houses and a burgeoning middle class all offering positions for local girls. There were traditional roles too for women on the farms and for single women to teach in schools. Women from the area were also employed in factories, for instance at the Cobra Works in Bushey, or making cocoa at Dr Tibbles' Victoria Works at Callowland, where in 1903 two thirds of the 550 employees were female.

Work of this nature was usually reserved for single women, it being expected that women should give up work once they married. The Post Office even required women employees to resign on marriage and forbade the hiring of married women for established positions. The War not only brought older women back into the workforce, it also made a wider range of roles available to them and opened up opportunities within industries that had previously been male preserves. Female workers took on more physically demanding jobs and responsible clerical jobs needed filling. The number of women in the Civil Service increased from 33,000 in 1911 to 102,000 by 1921.

There was increased pressure too on the professions to allow women in, with the result that medicine in particular saw the number of women practitioners rise by 150 per cent between 1914 and 1915 and double the following year. The overall number of women in work rose from 3.2 million to 5 million during the War, which chimed in with the ongoing fight for women's suffrage. One of the significant consequences of increased female participation in the workforce was a general rise in women's wages. Many former domestic workers found more rewarding employment in the factories, with the result that the employment of servants became much less viable – another factor in the post-war decline of the country house.

When hostilities began, Britain was totally unprepared for a Continental land war. The small, highly trained, professional standing army had previously been used mainly for policing the widely scattered Empire. It lacked the numbers and the equipment for large-scale fighting against the far bigger European armies. Although Britain was a leading manufacturing country, its industries were almost entirely concerned with peacetime production and deficient in machinery for the production of rifles, machine-guns and heavy artillery.

At the end of 1914, the BEF had an acute shortage of heavy guns and an inadequate supply of both light and heavy ammunition. To address this problem, Lloyd George's Ministry of Munitions introduced the Munitions of War Act on 26 May 1915. This emergency legislation was designed to increase Government control over the direction of the war effort. The Act gave the Ministry the power to: convert existing factories to wartime production under the direct control of the Government; control wages and working conditions for the duration; suspend trade union rights; and make strikes illegal in all factories engaged on war work. Disputes were to be settled by arbitration; despite this no other Allied Power, apart from Russia, suffered as many wartime strikes as Britain.

Increased uncertainty had meant that by the end of 1914 businesses like John Dickinson's paper mills were obliged to seek protection, in the form of marine insurance and War Risks Insurance. Employers also made efforts to retain their best men and avoid staff shortages, resulting not only from enlistment but also from men being diverted into munitions work. The Ministry accepted Dickinson's application for a protection certificate as a controlled establishment. Being a controlled establishment affected the conditions of employment of the workforce. Female workers were drafted in to replaced men in the paper mills as far as possible, such as at Dickinson's Home Park Mill.

The paper mills also suffered from shortages of raw materials, as their supplies of German glue and colours ceased, and from restrictions on the importation of timber and wood pulp. In response, by August 1914, Dickinson's were already developing wood pulp manufacture at Croxley and wood plugs for shells were later made for the Ministry.

Some of the mills were eventually turned over to munitions. At Nash Mills overtime was worked mostly by female staff making trench bombs and small shells. The British Paper Co Ltd at Frogmore Mills, Apsley, made fuse boxes, food containers, cigarette boxes for the Army and Navy Canteen Board and propellant pins for the Stokes Gun, which first saw action at the Battle of Loos. Numerous other small factories throughout the area turned their expertise to war work.

Watford's location, with its proximity to good transport links, made it a prime site for purpose-built munitions factories and works, which had a significant impact on the town. Shells required casings and the explosives to fill and propel them and it was soon apparent that the Royal Factories, such as the one at Woolwich, could no longer cope with the demand. In July 1915 an extensive National Factories scheme was introduced, which included the building of Shell Factories, Explosive Factories and National Filling Factories.

By August James Gordon & Company Ltd were busy constructing His Majesty's Explosive Factory (HMEF) Watford on a sixty-one acre site. Completed in December and managed by Roburite & Ammonal Ltd, the works produced chemical munitions for shells from ammonal, a combination of ammonium nitrate and aluminium powder. When the price of aluminium became prohibitive they switched to producing amatol, a mixture of TNT and ammonium nitrate.

At the same time, between September and October, the National Trench Warfare Filling Factory (NTWFF), HM No. 24, under direct Government control and known locally as Watford No. 1 (Station Estate), was built on an adjacent twenty-acre site at the intersection of Balmoral Road and the St Albans branch line. It consisted of nineteen sheds for the filling and assembly of 20 and 50lb trench warfare bombs and fuses and the filling of chemical shell exploders. In 1917 its production included 113,342 rifle grenades, 390,035 2-inch trench mortar bombs and 438,007 Red and White Phosphorous and other 4-inch bombs, totalling £816,040 in value.

The following February, work began on a forty-acre site off Bushey Mill Lane on NTWFF, HM No. 25 (Watford No. 2, Callowland). Also under direct control, it opened in July with twenty-six filling sheds, some made of wood, a magazine (capacity 300 tons) and its own railway sidings with access to the main line to Euston.

Between July 1916 and March 1917, considerable money and effort continued to be spent on improving road and rail connections and buildings and equipment. Watford No. 2 produced heavy trench mortar bombs, trench mortar fuses and assembled chemical weapons. Over this period 222,041 M/M bombs, 2,930 20lb bombs and 3,031 3cwt bombs, totalling £2,017,910 in value, were filled. From January 1917, some work was taken over by the Greenford Chemical Shell Assembly Station.

The actual filling was a simple process but potentially very dangerous. It was mainly done by unskilled women workers over the age of twenty-one, popularly known as 'munitionettes'. Personal testimony records that, for many of the women, being involved in this kind of work was great fun and for recreation the girls of Watford Nos. 1 and 2 formed their own football teams.

A 1918 play, *Handmaidens of Death*, by Herbert Tremaine, the pen name of author Maude Deuchar who lived in Letchworth, reveals something of the life of the 'canaries'. Written in 1918, the action concerns the uneasy friendship of two middle class workers with three of their working class colleagues and their frustration at the lack of available men for single women. For amusement, they resort to tucking love messages to 'Fritz' into the shells they are making, resulting in a stark confrontation with the ghost of a dead German soldier.

However, those who worked as fillers faced the side-effect of toxic jaundice resulting from TNT poisoning. Apart from the many fatalities due to this condition, it turned the handlers' faces a bright yellow colour, earning them the nickname 'canaries'. Some workers' children were born with a yellow tinge to their skin, yet apparently with no other ill-effects. An anonymous letter of July 1917 to Louis Levey, the general manager of No. 2 Works, complained that the measures used to protect workers from the effects of the 'yellow powder' were being abused. The system, whereby the girls worked in shifts to minimize contact with TNT, was being undermined by the matron. She had been allowing 'favourites' not to work with the dangerous materials, whilst others were exposed to it for 'weeks and weeks' at a time.

Because of the Defence of the Realm Act, press censorship meant the populace would have been largely unaware of the more dramatic details of the dangers affecting local munitions workers. The *London Gazette* of 22 June 1917 gave some details when reporting the award of the Edward Medal Second Class to Robert John Kirkam, a Fourth Class Examiner in the Department of Munitions Inspection. On the 6 February, Kirkham was working in the filling shed at No. 1 Works when he noticed smoke coming from a 4-inch Stokes bomb. With 'commendable presence of mind and courage he picked up the bomb, threw it out of the shed and shut the door'. The bomb exploded in the open with considerable violence but his swift action had saved many lives, as there were 50 workers in the shed at the time.

The events of the following October, when three workers at the same factory were not so fortunate, were not reported in the *Watford Observer* until long after the War (February 1920). Twenty-three-year-old Clara Frost of Ebury Road was working on the final shell assembly, soldering the cordite firing pins into the shells with a naked flame, when her soldering iron ignited the cordite on one of the shells. There was an explosion and Clara and two men standing nearby, Frederick Turner and Charles F. Tolfray, were blown up and the building engulfed in flames.

That same year the Watford Manufacturing Company, producers of jellies, egg powder, baking powder, pudding powder, and makers of

Dr Tibbles' Vi-Cocoa, had turned its Victoria Works over to munitions. In September, a fire broke out in a storeroom containing dried milk, nuts, advertising material and a consignment of Vi-Cocoa about to be dispatched to the troops. Luckily firefighters were able to bring the blaze under control before it caused serious damage. The following August the company was advertising in the *Watford Observer* for female workers aged between seventeen and twenty-five to join their 'Saw Mill' at Delectaland, where according to a 1910 advertisement, 'the Spirit of Delecta – symbol of wholesome purity' had previously produced chocolate and Vi-Cocoa.

Other established Watford firms were also drafted in to help the war effort. The Speedometer and Magneto Works on Whippendell Road produced magnetos for motor and aeroplane engines, such as the Vickers Vimy, a twin-engine biplane heavy bomber designed to attack targets in Germany. The plane did not become fully operational until the end of the War, however, but a Vimy made the first transatlantic flight in 1919.

Messrs Nicole Nielsen & Co based in Soho, had a factory in Watford, which also produced instruments for motorcars and shortly afterwards the very first flight instruments, including tachometers and magnetos. In 1914, when it was taken over by the government to help with the war effort, the company changed their name to the less Germanic-sounding 'North & Co'.

Local printing companies also found their services in demand. The cost of the War had made the circulating of gold currency prohibitive, so the Permanent Secretary to the Treasury, Sir John Bradbury, decided to replace coins with paper currency. Unfortunately, the initial paper notes proved easy to forge and the Treasury asked David Greenhill of the Bushey Colour Press (acquired by Andre, Sleigh and Anglo Engraving Co in 1914) to solve the problem. Greenhill's team developed a new way of engraving and printing a banknote which was difficult to photograph and therefore to forge. The 10s and £1 notes were printed by Waterlow and Sons Ltd in Milton Street, Callowland. When the Bank of England gained a legal monopoly on the issue of banknotes in 1921, the resulting loss of the contract contributed to the closure of the Waterlow and Sons works.

Labour shortages provided the unions with opportunities to increase their membership. In 1914 The National Union of Paper Workers was formed (an amalgamation of The National Amalgamated Society of Printers' Warehousemen and Cutters with the National Union of Paper Mill Workers) and meetings and recruitment drives were held at Dickinson's in April 1915. The Union took advantage of the shortages at Home Park Mill to press for higher wages. In June 1914, just prior to the outbreak of war, there had been unrest at Dickinson's Croxley Mill. The management, under pressure to maintain good relations with their workforce, acceded to the workers' demands, raising wages twice in seven months in 1917. A policy of War Bonuses was introduced, which the Union demanded should be added to the standard rates as a permanent wage. This had the effect of compressing the differential in pay between the labourers and yardmen and the machine and beater men, whose wages rose proportionally less. The company also seems to have been generous, giving gifts to staff to ease the burden of the War.

The War had consequences for another industrial campaign run by the Early Closing Association. The Association, which had the support of Queen Mary's brother, the Duke of Teck, aimed to reduce hours for shop workers. On 1 May 1914 he wrote to the *Daily Telegraph* calling for £5,000 to provide relief for 'thousands of young men and women who are at work in shops from eight to nine o'clock in the morning until nine or ten o'clock at night and later on Fridays and Saturdays, while many are not even free on Sunday mornings'. He went to cite the detrimental effects of overwork on health, personal development and family life.

By November 1917 the *Watford Observer* was able to report that with the streets darkened for fear of air raids and the 'withdrawal of nearly all male assistants from shops', the pre-war average opening times of 72 hours per week was no longer tenable. It went on to applaud the reduction in opening times within the retail trade to 48 hours, excluding staff meal breaks, yet, felt that this would be a temporary arrangement. When the 'boys' returned from the Front they would 'expect and deserve working hours of this description, as they remember only too well the few opportunities they had in the past for open air exercise and enjoyment'.

The imposition of Military Service caused instances of unnecessary individual hardship, particularly for small businesses. To highlight the absurdity of the authorities' rigid application of the rules, Major Bowden, MP for North-East Derbyshire, brought one such case to the attention of the House of Commons on 19 March 1918. According to Bowden, a master baker from St Albans had:

> *probably one of the biggest, if not the biggest, businesses of its kind in the city. He employed several hands; he was taken away, and the whole matter of his business was left in the hands of his young wife, an extremely delicate woman, and totally unfit to attempt to begin to manage a business ...* [the] *poor woman having to strive, literally night and day, alone, to cope with the filling in of the various forms required by the Ministry of Food. At that very time the husband, I hear, was cutting the grass round the officers' mess where he was stationed at Aldershot.*

At this time the Watford Tradesmen Association also reported that the shortage of labour and the lack of transport was creating difficulties in the delivery of goods around the area.

The public sector was affected as well as the private. Watford Post Office lost twenty-six of their postmen within the first week of the war, as they were either called up in the Regular Forces or with the Territorials. Postwomen took the place of the men, as did female ticket collectors at Watford Junction. Schools and caring institutions lost staff. Local doctors went to serve at the Front. Hemel Hempstead Joint Isolation Hospital lost its Medical Officer, Dr Gilbert Burnet, while Dr Young, of Gilroy and Young, also did military service.

At the beginning of the war Leavesden Asylum took on temporary staff and ten working patients, who were transferred from Darenth Asylum in Kent. By 1918 staff shortages had become so acute that three wards had to be closed, decreasing the number of patients to 1,767. They were not reopened until 1921. Women replaced male staff at the asylum as clerks, farm workers and as kitchen staff. Nurses were allowed to work on male TB wards for the first time. Nurses married to servicemen were allowed to stay on, whereas previously they had been forced to resign on marriage. Some of the temporary staff members were made permanent, in spite of being over forty and part-time staff were employed for the first time in 1918. In 1917 the salary of farm bailiffs was increased to encourage them to stay and they were allowed to develop the farms as they chose, with the advice of experts from the Wye Agricultural College.

In the Church, not only were the congregations called away but also members of the clergy who felt they could serve the cause better elsewhere, often as army chaplains. In 1916, St Mary's Hemel Hempstead lost its curate, the Rev G.A.C. Smith, who was followed in January 1917 by the Rev L. Gee, its vicar and the Methodist circuit minister the Rev T. Tiplady, who penned the following lines published in the *Gazette* on 30 January 1915:

'The Dying Soldier'

Mother dear I'm coming home,
Coming home to die,
From the land beyond the foam
Where the death bolts fly.

O'er the water I shall sail,
Dover's cliffs shall see,
There within our own sweet vale
You will bury me.

Mother, weep not for your boy,
Did I shun the fight?
Let them weep that have no joy
In their sons tonight.

In my bed of khaki clay
Sweetly I shall lie
As the lads in khaki may
Who for England die.

In 1916, Frederick Oliver Houseman, the vicar of St Mary's, Apsley End became an army chaplain. His curate the Rev James Herbert Reginald Lendrum followed him and was posted to the 8th King's Own (Royal Lancaster Regiment) in France. Lendrum was killed by a shell, along with three others, whilst he conducted a burial service on 22 August 1918. The Vicar of Aldenham, Kenneth Francis Gibbs served as Army Chaplain to the Hertfordshire Yeomanry between 1914 and

1921. His son, Leonard Charles Michael, was a Lieutenant in the Coldstream Guards.

The Rev R. Lee James of St Mary's Parish Church, Watford, a chaplain to the Territorial Army, had six of his sons serving either in the army or the navy. Amongst them Lieutenant Edmund Lee James was with the British Expeditionary Force contingent which arrived in France on 22 August 1914. He was followed by Cyril Henry Leigh James, a career soldier who later became a Brigadier-General in the Northumberland Fusiliers, commanding a unit there from April 1915 to May 1916. After a spell in Ireland, Cyril was back in France in March 1917, leading his men at the Battles of the Menin Road Ridge, Polygon Wood and Cambrai.

The Police

In Hertfordshire, eighty-five regular police officers left the force to join the services. Nine were killed and many more were injured, including Charles Frank Randall, who lost an arm. Despite this he later went on to become the Deputy Chief Constable. Even the wartime Chief Constable, Alfred Law, was recalled to the army in 1915, where he was promoted to Lieutenant-Colonel.

The shortfall in police manpower was compensated for through the recruitment of some 3,000 Special Constables. At the County Court in Watford, a hundred men were sworn in on the first Saturday of the war. Their duties included guarding vulnerable points, such as Watford Gas Works, Colne Valley Pumping Station, Bushey Heath Reservoir, and the L&NWR Pumping Station. The Special Constables wore white armbands when on duty. When required it was the job of these police volunteers to ensure that blackout restrictions were in force.

The shortage of men also prompted calls for women to be recruited into the police, with limited success in Hertfordshire. The Women's Police Volunteers, later renamed the Women's Police Service in 1915, was set up by Margaret Daimer Dawson with a particular view to curb the behaviour of the numerous young women set free by the new opportunities of wartime and save them from the risks of drunkenness, loose morals and crime. Eventually, from initially being responsible for the welfare of Belgian refugees in London, they began to be recruited in many other cities. The Ministry of Munitions used the WPS to supervise and search women in factories. Most of the 1,000 women who were trained came from socially privileged backgrounds; they were unpaid and not sworn in as full members of local police forces.

The Fire Service

A co-ordinated national fire service was not introduced until 1938, up until which time there were between 1400 and 1500 municipal fire brigades run by local councils in the UK. Most firemen were volunteers and worked part-time and, like the police, many were called upon. John Parkin of Bushey Fire Brigade, a reservist, was among the first wave to be called upon. He joined his regiment, The Royal Horse Artillery, as a driver. The subsequent drain on manpower was so acute that the Chorleywood Brigade, then relying on a horse-drawn vehicle with a steam pump, nearly ceased to exist. Luckily they were only rarely needed during the War.

Auxiliary firemen were required to fill the gaps. In Bushey, Rev Montague Hall and Rev H.C. Richardson were amongst those manning the pumps. Other, perhaps more suitable candidates were recruited from amongst retired firemen and local men with qualifications as surveyors and engineers. The latter were used for their experience in a supplementary role and to protect arsenals and government establishments. A number of Works had their own fire fighting teams, including Sedgwick's Brewery in Watford.

In 1914, the Watford Fire Brigade consisted of twenty-four men led by Captain R.A. Thorpe and Superintendent H.M. Pratchett. They all lived within easy reach of the fire station, which was located in the High Street, enabling them to respond to a call in as little as half a minute. The station had two fire engines, No. 1 Engine for use in town and No. 2 for use outside the Watford area. Once the engines were on their way, anyone not already on board followed by bicycle. Henry Pratchett had served at sea and during his twelve previous years' experience in Tottenham, he had been recommended three times for life-saving. Superintendent from 1910 to 1929 he was instrumental in the introduction of motor-driven fire engines to Watford in 1913. In contrast, the Hemel Hempstead Fire Station still had a horse-drawn engine until 1917.

On the morning of Tuesday, 13 February 1917, Watford Fire Brigade was called out to what was officially reported in the *Watford Observer* as a 'small fire … at a factory in Hertfordshire'. The fire was actually at a munitions factory, Watford No. 1 in Bushey Mill Lane, just beyond Watford Station, and the rapidly spreading flames had already begun to threaten many of the adjacent buildings. Because of the strict censorship in force few details were recorded in the newspapers at the time. The fire had broken out in a powder mixing room, where explosive powder was processed in a mixing machine. Local fire fighters, with the aid of the Watford Brigade, and teams from the Victoria Works, the Council and Messrs Sedgewick's, marshalled the 'hundreds of girls' employed there off the premises, helped by constables and 'specials' who controlled the traffic.

Superintendent Prachett was first on the scene, along with Firemen Fountain and Wise and Driver Robinson. Told that it was imperative to stop the fire from spreading to the adjoining buildings, the Watford Brigade distinguished itself by soon getting the fire under control. Prachett was the first to carry out a case of TNT from the burning building and his men removed the rest, assisted by the works brigade. Due to their swift action only two workmen with burns, Charles Moorcroft, a licensed victualler from Harpenden, and William Pride, a shopkeeper living in Percy Road, Watford, were taken to the district hospital, where they died later of shock. Several others were injured.

After the incident the Watford firemen were invited to the Council Chamber, where Lord Clarendon thanked them for their bravery, but they did not receive official recognition until after the War. Only then it was acknowledged that there had also been an explosion in the No. 2 Filling Works. However, Superintendent Pratchett, Firemen Fountain, Wise and Robinson were awarded their Order of the British Empire medals on 10 November 1920, in the Clarendon Road Drill Hall Yard, by Brigadier-General Viscount Hampden, the Lord Lieutenant of the county, for, as the *Watford Observer* put it, their 'conspicuous courage and devotion to duty on the occasion of a fire at a munitions factory'.

Daniel Fountain, who lived in Beechen Grove, was an original member of the Watford Local Board of Health Fire Brigade, formed in 1888. He was awarded the Long Service Silver Medal in 1918. When he retired from the fire brigade, he became the deputy mace-bearer for the town council. Richard Wise lived in Watford High Street and had been taken on to help fill the vacancies caused by firemen being away on active service. F.J. Foxen also received an OBE, presumably for the same incident, during which his 'great courage and devotion to duty ... was considered to have prevented a most serious loss of life'.

The No. 1 Works Fire Brigade also received official recognition in the *London Gazette* (22 June 1917). The Chief of the Factory Police and Fire Superintendent Thomas Luther Burt received the Edward Medal Second Class, for the courageous rescue of the two workers. In the *Gazette* account, at about 11.20 am, Burt was doing his rounds when he heard a slight booming noise from No 2 mixing house. He immediately ran out two lines of hose. The flash had knocked the foreman into a doorway, where he was staggering about, so dazed he did not know what had happened. Burt then:

> *rushed into the building, which was burning fiercely and full of suffocating smoke. He carried out Mixer Price* [sic] *and immediately returned to rescue Mixer Morecroft* [sic], *the smoke by then being so dense and the heat so great that he was compelled to crawl along on his hands and knees before he could reach Morecroft. Afterwards he worked hard in the removal of explosives from the building.*

In the packing room adjoining the mixing house were stacked tons of high explosive, which, had the flames reached them, could have destroyed half the town.

On a pitch black and stormy evening the following September, the Watford Brigade was called out again to deal with the storeroom blaze at the Victoria Works (see p.72). The nature of the items that had caught fire brought back memories of a similar blaze in 1903, which had destroyed a greater part of the works. Hundreds of people rushed over to Callowland to witness the flames, which were dramatically illuminated by flashes of lightning. Despite fears that the strong wind would whip up the fire, Captain Bruce of the Works Brigade and Captain Thorpe and Superintendent Prachett of the Watford Council Brigade, (assisted by the Croxley Mills Brigade, Messrs Sedgewick's and Bushey Brigades), had the fire under control within an hour. Their 'superhuman' effort saved the adjoining main building and the Freeman Factory from destruction. Only slight injuries were sustained and after a fifteen-hour shift without rest, the workers were able to return to work the next morning.

Schools

Schools during wartime provided no refuge for pupils from the world outside; private and state schools were affected alike. Gadesbridge House in Hemel Hempstead, acquired from the Paston Cooper family in 1914 to become Gadebridge Park School, was immediately turned into a temporary army camp. As with the St Albans schools mentioned previously (see p.58), school holidays were disrupted. The Royal Caledonian School in Bushey, started term late simply because it had also been considered for military requisition. Many of the teachers had joined up and the staff shortages were filled where possible by supply teachers or married women returning to teaching.

Teaching was not an exempted profession and Ashfield School, Bushey, had its first assistant, J.T.H. Smith called up. Similar call ups aroused protest, to little avail, in Watford and Chipperfield. Not only the teaching staff were affected; the enlistment of nurses undermined the efficiency of the school medical service. The turnover in staff was particularly felt in boys' schools and the larger mixed schools, with the inevitable impact on standards.

Elementary education was subordinated to the needs of the War and school attendance plummeted. Hundreds of older children worked on farms, in factories and in shops to offset the lack of adults. Those still in school were used to promote the war effort: cultivating 'war gardens', knitting and making jams and pickles for economy and producing thousands of garments and other goods for the Red Cross and the army. At Merry Hill Junior School, Bushey, the girls were put to knitting socks, mittens, helmets and scarves for the soldiers, shirts for the Red Cross and blankets for the Serbian Relief Organization.

As the War progressed, these efforts became more industrial in nature and any notional educational value was increasingly sidelined. The Technical Centre in St Albans produced arm splints, crutches and stretchers for the Red Cross and hand grenade boxes for the Ministry of Munitions. In Hertfordshire, links were formed between schools and munitions factories in the region, providing technical training for older elementary school boys, so that pupils could eventually take up semi-skilled posts.

Hertfordshire County Council encouraged child labour to such an extent that that the Board of Education was forced to remonstrate.

Parents were obliged to send their children to school between the age of five and fourteen at this time, but in agricultural areas of Hertfordshire an exemption could be made if a child was over twelve and had passed the Fifth Grade prescribed by the Elementary Code. In the urban districts of Barnet, Bushey, East Barnet and Watford, the higher Sixth Standard had to be attained before exemption. An agricultural byelaw of 1899 also allowed children over eleven who had passed the Fourth Standard, to be employed full-time on farms during harvest time, as long as they attended 250 sessions between October and June. They were not entitled to full exemption until the age of thirteen.

Pressure was exerted by employers, councillors, and even the press, to ease restrictions and take children out of school to fill labour shortages in both industry and agriculture, with the result that absenteeism increased. In March 1915 Watford Labour Exchange estimated that farmers were, on average, almost one hand short per farm. Hertfordshire had the third highest exemption figures in England and Wales. By 1916 it was estimated that farms around Watford and Hemel Hempstead were operating on half their manpower. Despite calls for increased relaxation of the rules, the local education authority felt that there were many abuses regarding the nature of the work children were allowed to do. Boys from St Albans exempted for farm work were found to be working in factories and shops, and even as odd-job hands at Mill Hill School, a local public school. In Hemel Hempstead, many parents believed that 80 per cent school attendance was acceptable. After 1916 a change in attitudes brought a decline in the number of exemptions.

Shortages of materials hit schools as well as businesses and homes, and economies had to be made. Heating was a problem in winter, with freezing classrooms due to the shortage of coal and paraffin. In January 1915, Ashfield School in Bushey nearly ran out of coal. By Spring 1917, the pupils of the nearby London Road School were also suffering, but Merry Hill Infants School was forced to close. Two years later, both the Merry Hill Infants and Junior School were closed. The lack of wood pulp meant a return to using slates instead of paper. Other general shortages also led to children being encouraged to collect local alternatives, where available. For instance, in response to the lack of imported animal feed in 1918 the pupils of King's Langley collected

90 bushels of acorns, and hunting for blackberries for jam became an obsession across the county.

Dates in the calendar and points on the map took on new meanings within the schoolroom. History and Geography lessons provided opportunities to reflect on the context and course of the war, and national days were celebrated with new vigour. On Trafalgar Day, 21 October 1914, the pupils of Callow Land CC Boys School in Leavesden Road, Watford, sung 'The Marseillaise', neatly commemorating a past victory and a current alliance at the same time. Every senior school had a Cadet Corps. At Watford Grammar, boys aged between twelve and eighteen joined a Corps and the unit was recognized as being affiliated to the 1st Battalion of the Hertfordshire Regiment in February 1915.

All school pupils had links with the war through the involvement of relatives, friends, ex-pupils and ex-teachers in the forces. As updates were given in the press about the recruitment of ex-students, additions were made to schools' Rolls of Honour. By October 1915, the *Watford Observer* published the London Orphan School Roll of Honour, which by then had seventeen names, with six killed in action. In Bushey, Ralph James, the Head of Ashfield, prepared a roll of Old Boys who had enlisted, including his two sons: Cyril with the Army Service Corps and Ralph with the Royal Irish Fusiliers; one son was wounded in France. The *Watford Observer* reported that hundreds of former pupils had joined from the local elementary schools, commenting that 'nothing gives the teachers more pleasure than to see a smart young fellow in khaki'.

Lewis Jones (1894–1953), a former pupil, of Callow Land CC, interrupted his promising career to enlist with the London Regiment, The Queen's Westminster Rifles in December 1914. He left school in 1908, aged fourteen, to study design at Watford School of Science and Art. Two years later he joined the Silver Studio, the internationally renowned textile and wallpaper designers in Hammersmith, London, to become a designer of furnishing and dress fabrics. He fought on the Front Line in France and the Salonica Campaign against the Bulgarians, before he was wounded in the head by a Turkish sniper. Jones was found by Nomadic Arabs, who dressed his wounds, during which time his parents received a 'Missing believed killed' telegram.

He returned to Front Line duty in Palestine and Jordan, and in June

1918 he was sent to the Western Front where, at Seaforth Farm near Messines, north-west of Lille, the regiment took heavy casualties. As senior NCO Acting Sergeant, Jones led the remaining troops for which he was awarded the Military Medal. After the war he returned to Watford to marry and resumed his career at the Silver Studio, becoming the principal artist and designer.

As local families began to suffer losses, elementary schools began honouring the fallen in the manner of public schools and collections were made for the wounded. Ex-pupils now serving and other soldiers would visit schools and tell something of their experiences and the schoolchildren would correspond with them and send gifts in return. At a time when Watford Grammar School for Boys was expanding to include a sixth form, 645 ex-members of staff and boys served in the war effort, 97 of whom lost their lives while on active service as far afield as China, including ten lost at the Battle of the Somme. A number were also decorated, among them Thomas William Heather, who received the MC and bar, and Alan Rice Oakley who gained the DFC. Of the 575 alumni of Aldenham School who joined up 26 were killed and 10 decorated.

Girls' schools were not exempt from the military atmosphere. In Chapel at Abbots Hill, a recently established independent school for girls near Hemel Hempstead, Miss Katrine read out the names of fathers and brothers serving at the Front; these were soon followed by the news of the casualties. The Roll of Honour, painted in 1917, still hangs in the school. A plaque also commemorates John Reginald Noble Graham, the father of a pupil, Lesley Graham, who won the VC in 1918. In the spring term of 1916 Miss Dewar recorded that the mistresses all adopted a type of uniform made of navy-blue serge, a measure perhaps brought on by wartime economy, which some of the pupils thought made them look like 'lift-boys'.

Health

Full employment and higher wages meant that some working class families were better off in 1915 than before the War. Malnutrition, however, still existed in the slum areas of Watford and St Albans, to which the persistence of tuberculosis was a contributory factor. An increase in vermin was also recorded and by 1916 more children attended school in a 'neglected condition'. The disruptions of the War were blamed for these rising levels of squalor. The billeting of soldiers in family homes and war work were held responsible for distracting mothers from the care of their children, while the rise in truancy and disruptive behaviour was ascribed to the lack of a father figure in many households.

By 1915 the Director of the NSPCC had already addressed a meeting in Watford stressing the importance of health care and the need for State participation. In 1914 voluntary groups had filled the gaps, providing school meals in Watford, and local education authorities were permitted to provide children with meals during school holidays, but by 1917 the effects of food shortages began to take their toll. Malnourishment had long existed in the more deprived urban schools, and as yet there was still no policy of state provision for free school meals.

The poor health of many army recruits highlighted the growing problem and towards the end of the War improvements in health care became a priority, partly in response to the need for 'fit and hardy men', but also as a reaction to the increasing public awareness of social neglect and poor childcare. In June 1917 the Duchess of Marlborough gave a speech at a garden party in Watford in which she railed against the prevailing inadequate housing and poverty. The Earl of Clarendon too linked the rejection of a million recruits with the 500,000 children leaving school each year with untreated physical defects. In response Watford Council supported a 'semi-official' health and welfare clinic.

At the beginning of the War Hertfordshire had more school medical staff than any other county, but again enlistment put pressure on the School Medical Service. As the War progressed there was a shortage of nurses, as many volunteered for nursing work with the troops overseas and in military hospitals on the Home Front. In 1915 Hemel Hempstead's nurse volunteered for service overseas. Over the following eighteen months her four replacements each served briefly before moving on. Constant changes of staff occurred in Watford, St Albans and Barnet, affecting the level of health care provision. The County Superintendent of Nurses reported in 1916 that inspections were being ignored and just over a quarter of ailments were being treated.

By 1917 there were slight improvements, but the prevailing mood was that the State should take more responsibility. In 1918 Hertfordshire Education Committee adopted a scheme of clinics providing dental and health care for minor ailments, maternity care and welfare at a number of centres throughout the county, including Hemel Hempstead, St Albans and Watford, with outlying districts served by travelling clinics. Parents would pay half the cost towards refraction work and spectacles and local hospitals provided treatment for enlarged tonsils and adenoids. Arrangements were made with London hospitals for the X-ray treatment of ringworm. Slowly progress was made, the 1918 Education Act guaranteeing elementary schoolchildren easier access to the health services recommended in their medical examinations.

Leisure

During the War organised sport suffered. At first it was felt inappropriate to continue major sporting activities and, as the young and fit heeded the call to enlist, sport lost its best to the services. At a local level there were numerous clubs across a range of sports, including popular team sports such as football and cricket, but also athletics, bowls and hockey. Football controversially continued until the close of the 1914–15 season, with Watford FC as the Southern League champions. League football was then discontinued until 1919. In 1915 a number of leading clubs within the South formed a regional league, the London Combination, and Watford competed.

The London Combination League: 1915–16 Season							
	PL	W	D	L	GF	GA	PTS
1. Chelsea	22	17	3	2	71	18	37
2. Millwall	22	12	6	4	46	24	30
3. Arsenal	22	10	5	7	43	46	25
4. West Ham Utd	22	10	4	8	47	35	24
5. Fulham	22	10	4	8	45	37	24
6. Tottenham Hotspur	22	8	8	6	38	35	24
7. Brentford	22	6	8	8	36	40	20
8. Queens Park Rangers	22	8	3	11	27	41	19
9. Crystal Palace	22	8	3	11	35	55	19
10. Watford	22	8	1	13	37	46	17
11. Clapton Orient	22	4	6	12	22	44	14
12. Croydon Common	22	3	5	14	24	50	11

The season finished in January and Watford then competed in a supplementary expanded competition of fourteen teams coming seventh. The following year the club resigned, or was 'excluded', according to the *Watford Observer,* along with a number of other clubs without all the outstanding fixtures being played. To make matters worse, the West Herts Club and Ground also declined to rent them the ground, because of declining support and opposition to professional football. In consequence, the directors of Watford FC suspended operations 'until more propitious times'. Normal peacetime competitions were resumed in 1919, when only goal average deprived Watford of a second consecutive Southern League championship.

On 16 June 1915, the *Watford Observer* published a list of Hertfordshire footballers who had joined up. From a hundred clubs 1,407 men joined. The clubs listed were local amateur clubs, but the numbers would have made meaningful competition difficult. Whole teams joined, as in the case of the twelve members of the Watford Orient 1st team. Sixteen joined from Elstree and forty-three from Leaveden Asylum. Some were works teams and social clubs, others church teams, as in the case of St John's Church, Watford, and St Peter's and St Saviour's, St Albans or the YMCA. The LNWR team in Watford supplied thirty-six volunteers, while Croxley and Croxley North End Juniors lost forty-five. A Watford and District League continued, in which small and junior teams competed.

First-class cricket was entirely abandoned for the whole of the War, and the remaining 1914 season fixtures were scrapped. Hertfordshire Cricket Club was placed second in the unfinished Minor Counties Championship for the 1914 season; the last matches being played on 25 August, the championship then being discontinued until 1920. Cricket did not entirely fade away during the War, however. It was still played in Britain's schools and universities and by army teams, but club cricket suffered, with little or none played and grounds becoming neglected. Typically, many sportsmen were in the Territorials, and teams like Hemel Hempstead Cricket Club, which had two players in 'F' Company of the Hertfordshire Regiment in 1914, lost members.

Almost every village or factory had a team, but by 1916 club cricket in the South of England went into serious decline and many clubs were closed down indefinitely. Before the end of the War, efforts were made for revival in order to boost morale, but many village teams did not resume playing until well after the Armistice. Shenley Cricket Club, who played against local rivals, London Colney and Radlett, managed to field teams from its inception in 1861 until August 1914. The August Bank Holiday weekend was due to be their last match, against Arkley, but was never played. The club was reformed in 1921.

Radlett Club's hopes of repeating the successes of 1913, their best pre-War season were also cut short. Poor St Stephen's (near St Albans) were thrashed once again in the penultimate game before war broke out, but then the club records record, 'The grass grew on the out-field of the cricket ground and the wicket was no longer cut and tended and so for those dark years Newberries Ground continued to slumber.' After five long years, the ground had turned into a meadow and money had to be raised to revive the club. Despite many members joining up and the loss of their ground in September 1914, that December Bushey Cricket Club voted to stay in existence.

Bowling was another popular sport in the early twentieth century, with a number of clubs springing up in the region, the sport appealing to a younger age group. Upton Road Bowling Club, founded in 1912, was renamed the Watford Bowling Club, and moved to Cassiobury Park in 1922. Upton had matches with their Hemel Hempstead counterparts, but the depletion of members and ground staff due to active service meant a slow lapse in activity until peacetime.

Even an activity as harmless as gardening was affected. The Bushey and Bushey Heath Cottage Gardening Society (founded 1900) was suspended in 1916. Despite restrictions, other leisure activities continued as normally as was possible. The annual round of calendar festivities, fêtes and circuses included: May Day, celebrated in King's Langley with its May Day garland and May Queen doll; Hemel Hempstead's Great Statue Fair and Hospital Sunday parade; a fundraiser for the West Herts Hospital held in September; and Bostock Wombwell's Menagerie with its elephants, which visited Watford in December.

Cinemas were already a major attraction in most towns by 1914. Watford boasted the Kinetic in the Corn Exchange, the Electric Coliseum in St Albans Road, the Empire Picture Palace (renamed the ABC and later the Cannon) in Merton Road, and the Cinema Palace, the town's first purpose-built cinema, at the junction of High Street and King Street, from 1910 to 1915. The Central Hall in King Street, later named the Regal, then the Essoldo and finally becoming a bingo hall, opened in 1913. The Carlton, built in 1910 and converted to a cinema in 1921, was originally the Clarendon Road (roller) Skating Rink. It was also used to stage boxing matches, local lightweights Phil Norwood, Sid George and Harry Smith battling it out there during 1914.

In the first weeks of the war cinema audience numbers fell. In response, the Electric Cinema branded itself the 'the patriotic theatre' and began showing 'war news as it arrives'. By 1915 the cinemas had started showing films that were more related to current events, like *A Daughter of Belgium,* with the subtitle, 'a vivid and sensational tale of modern times', which was shown at the Electric Coliseum in January. Things had moved on two years later, when the main feature was *The Battle of the Ancre and the Advance of the Tanks,* advertised as being 'far ahead of *The Battle of the Somme*'. Censored by General Headquarters so that nothing could be called a fake, the film featured 'pictures actually taken on the battlefield'. *The Battle of the Ancre* was particularly resonant for local audiences because of the involvement of the Hertfordshire Regiment.

By February 1918 the appeal of war-related stories was well established, with the Americans providing the topical escapism of *Pearl of the Army* and *Behind the Lines,* 'a powerful military drama' set in revolutionary Mexico, while at the Central Hall cinema-goers could catch 'Pathé's great masterpiece *Patra* being the first episode of *The Fighting Chammys'* or '*With our French Allies No.2*: showing the work of our brave ally *Behind the Lines'.*

In the cinemas the British Pathé newsreels, the Pathé Animated Gazettes, provided the newspapers with competition. In Britain propaganda film-making lagged behind that of the German film industry. The attempt by The British Actors Film Company in Bushey to put its expertise to use for propaganda films failed, but in 1916 *The Battle of the Somme,* a Government-backed documentary, set a new standard. Purporting to portray the reality of the trenches, it played to sell-out audiences nationwide. Mixing genuine footage with staged battle scenes (some realities were too visceral), it proved a great success, and further documentary style films followed.

In the meantime the Ideal Film Company based at the Elstree Studios, Borehamwood, was busy producing escapist fare such as *Lady Windermere's Fan* (1916), based on Oscar Wilde's play; *Justice* (1917), a crime thriller by John Galsworthy; *Tom Jones* (1917), the Henry

Fielding classic; and the drama *Red Pottage* (1918). Towards the end of the War they brought out a timely biopic, *The Life Story of David Lloyd George* (1918). Despite this activity, the British film industry lost ground during the War to the more advanced and popular American imports, almost grinding to a halt as a result.

The stage, meanwhile, offered an alternative to the new realism. The Palace Theatre, Watford, had opened in 1908 as the Watford Palace of Varieties, featuring a mix of variety, Music Hall and Pantomime at Christmas. In the early days the shows were imported from other theatres and performers came up from London, such as the Music Hall actor and composer Herbert Shelley. By 1914, horizons were broadened and local audiences could enjoy the best of musical theatre and performances of works by Shakespeare.

In August 1914 the *Blinders of Virtue* was playing, with the 'latest war news' shown between performances and Special Military Performances were introduced before the advertised programme. From 1915 there was a greater emphasis on plays and when Grand Opera came to town any anti-German feeling was evidently put to one side. Audiences were presented with programmes that included *Tannhauser* by Richard Wagner (1813–1883); the German themed *The Bohemian Girl* by the Irish composer Michael William Balfe (1808–1870); and *The Count of Luxembourg,* an operetta by the Austro-Hungarian Franz Lehar (1870–1948).

Variety was not neglected, with appearances by the international Music Hall star Marie Lloyd and the comedian Fred Karno, who was instrumental in nurturing the talents of Charlie Chaplin and Stan Laurel. At the same time the overriding concerns of the moment were reflected in the growing number of plays with a military theme. Titles such as *In the Ranks* and *Chosen by the People*, which were described as 'Military Dramas', ran alongside the ever-popular musical comedies. Henry Baynton, who was to become a well-known Shakespearean actor and manager, made the first of his many visits to the theatre in Oscar Wilde's *The Importance of being Ernest.* The military theme carried on into 1918, with such titles as *The Pride of the Regiment, Seven Days' Leave, Married on Leave* and *Reported Missing.*

For those who wanted something less demanding there was Derby House, the property originally purchased by the Metropolitan Railway at 44 High Street, close to the junction with Clarendon Road, and intended to become the booking hall for their station. After this project fell through, the building was extensively refurbished in 1916, its frontage re-faced with the addition of two medallions of Queen Victoria and the rear garden opened up as The Empress Winter Gardens and Tea Lounge, providing a suitable venue for entertainment and refreshment.

The Local Press in Wartime

One direct outcome of the War was the launch of a new local paper, *The Watford Illustrated,* published by photographer and engraver Frederick Downer. The first issue, published on Thursday, 13 August 1914, set out the paper's aim to be 'an Illustrated Historical Record of local events during this grave crisis'. This it delivered with a patriotic flavour and extensive use of photographs at a time when most local newspapers contained very few. The new style, carrying few advertisements and little hard news, struck an immediate chord with the public, the first copy almost selling out. From then on it came out weekly on Saturdays, priced at 1d.

'We're well on our way/ In the Berlin Express./The Bulldog - he's going it fine,/You can see by his stride/ And the name on his side/ He's a winner, he'll break the line.' Private W. Hunter, 1/2 2nd London Regiment, (Watford Illustrated, December 1914)

The photographs of troops in the area and details of their units and movements were integral to its appeal, but by 22 August the *Watford Illustrated* was already courting official disfavour, being asked to 'refrain from giving particulars (…) as the War Office have requested the Press not to do so'.

The Watford Illustrated was providing new competition for the already well established *Watford Observer* and *The Watford Leader and West Herts News*. *The Watford Leader,* perhaps the most successful paper in West Herts, was founded in 1891 and printed by H.T. Gardiner of 101 the High Street. The older *Watford Observer* was first published on 24 January 1863, by Samuel Alexander Peacock to serve the areas of Watford, Bushey and Rickmansworth. By the early twentieth century, it had been renamed the *West Herts and Watford Observer*, having absorbed a number of other titles and now possessed a circulation that stretched as far as Harrow, St Albans, Tring, and Chesham.

The war proved a mixed blessing for these two local papers; while providing ample opportunities for dramatic content, there were difficulties with production. As the war progressed, censorship became more stringent and pictures and stories that might potentially disclose any military information were forbidden. As a result, *The Watford Illustrated* ceased publication on 22 February 1916, with the following 'Important Notice':

> *Owing to the enhanced price and great scarcity of paper, together with other difficult conditions, we are reluctantly compelled to cease publication of "Watford Illustrated" until such time as things become more normal.*

The Watford Leader had already closed in 1915, probably due to the effects of labour and paper shortages. Paper shortages also meant that the *Watford Observer* had to reduce its number of pages down to two, and its size to tabloid in March 1918.

The Press grabbed every opportunity to publish favourable portrayals of life at the Front. For instance, on 9 January 1915, the *Watford Observer* gave readers Percy Tarver's upbeat appraisal of Christmastime: 'we lived on the best of things – boiled fowls, potatoes, jam, beans, butter and rum'. However, details of engagements featuring

Hertfordshire Regiments were obliged by censorship rules to be generalised, and when casualty numbers were given, they were stated as vague, round numbers.

For the official information on the military, readers turned to the *London Gazette*, which supplied details of commissions, medals, and the fallen. As a counterblast to the authorized version, *The Hobocob*, was a journal published in 1917 by a Household Brigade Officer in the Cadet Battalion, based at Bushey Hall. A mix of serious pieces and poems interspersed with cartoons and comic articles, it has been described by Graham Seal, author of *The Soldiers' Press: Trench Journals in the First World War,* as being similar to other 'trench journals of the middling sort', like the *Wipers Times* and the *M+D* of the Canadian Field Ambulance. The *Hobocob* lampooned the advertisements in the *Gazette* and *The Dagger, or London in the Line* (quarterly of the 56 London Division) for instance those promoting self-improvement, such as 'Pelmanism', a then fashionable training system for the mind. Nevertheless, it also carried genuine advertising for the Criterion Restaurant, Gamages, and J. P. Taylor, a military tailor in Watford.

Some aspects of newspaper war reports had unforeseen repercussions. As a result of the anti-German sentiments expressed through the use of dachshunds in political cartoons, advertisements and postcards, it was reported that some of these unfortunate dogs had become the victims of hostility. The author Graham Greene, a schoolboy in Berkhamsted at the outbreak of the War, recorded the anti-German hysteria experienced in his hometown in his autobiography (*A Sort of Life*, 1971). During one incident a dachshund was reputedly stoned in the high street. Though reports of this kind have been repeated, and have entered into Great War folklore, there are few documented cases. But in restaurants sauerkraut and German sausage did come off the menus.

More significantly, people stranded on the wrong side of the border suffered. Rumours were everywhere, suggesting that numerous enemy aliens were at large and spies lurked in the shadows. Supposedly, there were several thousand aliens in the Watford area alone, according to the *Watford Observer* of 22 August 1914, and some genuine British citizens found themselves having to prove their identity. At the Watford Petty Sessions, a German resident of Queen's Road, Frank Kaver

Neumayer, was accused of failure to disclose his possession of firearms, which was now illegal under the Aliens' Registration Act, 1914. The court decided 'not to punish (him) with imprisonment but inflict a fine of £10'. They took into account his previous good character and the fact that he was a member of a local rifle club.

Even in the village of Abbots Langley, as the paper reported in October 1914, a suspected spy was arrested and sent to London for questioning. Lucy Kemp-Welch's Art School in Bushey was not exempt from scrutiny. It was closed in June 1915 when two students were accused of spying, after being found painting near Watford Bridge. The proprietor of Bushey Hall Hotel felt obliged to place an advertisement in the *Watford Observer* stating that there were no German or Austrian servants employed in the house.

Local Photographers
Photography was an important part of the growth of media coverage during the War and the *Watford Illustrated* encouraged contributions from local photographers throughout its short existence. Army and related military events unsurprisingly dominate the photographic

'A' Company marching along St Albans Road, Watford, at the end of July 1915, bound for Gallipoli. One of the shops on the other side of the road is the shop belonging to Harry Cull.

collections that survive from the period. A number of photographic studios existed in the area and they were eager to record significant moments, whether for public or private consumption.

From pictures postcards could be made and servicemen on the eve of departure or the wounded on their return sent cards to their families or friends as mementos, attempting to reassure them. Henry Robert Cull was a major local photographer and postcard seller who supplied images for the newspapers. Originally from Ventnor, on the Isle of Wight, he had been established in Watford for some years at 159 St Albans Road. He took many pictures of troops on the march passing through the town and postcards of posed groups of soldiers.

The large number of troops in the area provided business opportunities for other photographers, such as James Henry Lawrence and William Coles. Lawrence was a successful ex-gold prospector in Australia and New Zealand who had set up a series of photographic studios, first in Fulham and then in Watford. He had premises at 71 Queen's Road in 1914 and his Australian Studios at 110a High Street. Coles had his studio nearby at 16 Queens Road.

Meanwhile, W.H. Cox set up the Ricardo Studios at 'Grenfell',

Members of the Isle of Wight Rifles in Watford, by Harry Cull. (Courtesy of the Isle of Wight Family History Society)

Four new recruits from Watford, Photographed at Lawrence's Australian Studios

London Road, St Albans, where he produced 'high class portraiture'. By 1914 the studio had probably been taken over by Robert Catcheside who, as well as taking wedding groups, took a number of group photographs of wounded soldiers at the nearby Napsbury Hospital.

Civilians and the War Effort

While the young men volunteered for service at the Front, members of the civilian population also 'did their bit' by becoming involved in voluntary activities and organizations. Members of the local gentry saw it as their duty to galvanize the war effort on the Home Front, with the Hon Mrs Capell, Countess of Essex, prominent in setting the example. Adele Capell (née Adele Grant) was an American-born socialite who had married George Devereux de Vere Capell, the 7th Earl of Essex and the family lived in Watford at Cassiobury House. A society beauty, she had modelled for Hubert Von Herkomer's painting, *Lady in White.* She had two daughters, Lady Iris and Lady Joan, who also became involved in war work. Throughout the War the Countess promoted and supported various causes, working with the Queen Mary's Needlework Guild, the Urban Council for War Relief and becoming President of the Soldiers and Sailors Families Association.

Lucy Kemp-Welch put her talents to use as a propaganda artist. The most famous product of Herkomer's Art School, she had attended the school at the age of nineteen and went on to live for most of her life in Bushey. An ardent believer in painting out of doors, she became renowned for her depiction of horses and was the first President of the Society of Animal Painters. She followed in Herkomer's footsteps by setting up her own School of Animal Painting. Her illustrated edition of Anna Sewell's *Black Beauty* came out during the war in 1915. She

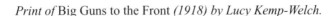

Print of Big Guns to the Front *(1918) by Lucy Kemp-Welch.*

had already painted propaganda pieces during the Boer War and again she put her skill at portraying horses in vigorous action at the service of the war effort.

One of Kemp-Welch's best paintings, *Forward the Guns*, was painted from studies she made with the assistance of the Commanding Officer of Bulford Camp on Salisbury Plain, where the artillery were on manoeuvres in 1917. According to her obituary in *The Times*, published 28 November 1958: 'For this picture she sat with her easel on Salisbury Plain while eight batteries of horse artillery were driven towards her so that she could sketch the general outline of their movement.'

Kemp-Welch exhibited other paintings on similar themes, notably *Big Guns to the Front* (National Museum of Wales) and *The Leaders of a Heavy Gun Team* (Royal Artillery Institution). With her sister, Edith, she also designed war recruitment posters. Her horse, Black Prince, who had posed for *Black Beauty*, now became the model for her war poster *Enlist Now*. She involved herself at a local level by designing posters for fundraising concerts.

Recruitment poster by Lucy Kemp-Welch. (Courtesy of the Bushey Museum and Art Gallery)

Her sister Edith's poster 'Remember Scarborough!' utilized the outrage felt by the British public after the indiscriminate shelling of the North East coast by the German Navy in December 1914, to encourage men to enlist. A sketch entitled 'Women's Work in the Great War' (now preserved in the Bushey Museum), depicting a female industrial worker at a lathe, shows that Lucy was also interested in the human impact of the War. As someone who was seen as a suffragist by the male dominated art establishment for battling to get her work exhibited, it is interesting that her greater unrealized ambition was that of serving abroad as a nurse, ambulance driver or war artist; something achieved by one of her former pupils, Lucy Lockwood, who was accepted as an ambulance driver.

Motor vehicles were still a relative luxury and 'Do not use a motor car for pleasure' was a slogan to be found written on walls around the country. Car owners in Watford responded, as elsewhere, by organizing a Volunteer Driver brigade. These Motor Volunteers were organised into a National Association and a Hertfordshire Corps was established in April 1915. In June the following year, William Joynson-Hicks, 1st Viscount Brentford and Conservative MP for the area, arguing in the House of Commons against an increase in Licence Duty on Motor Cars, pointed out that motorists were providing useful war work by using their vehicles to transport wounded personnel and thus saving the State great expense. He stated that in the previous twelve months, car owners in Hertfordshire had carried 6,000 cases to hospital, 18,000 cases between hospitals, plus 110,000 passengers.

Albert Ranney Chewett of Reveley Lodge, Bushey Heath, was one such car owner involved with the National Motor Volunteers. A man of inherited wealth, he had come from an influential family in Toronto, Canada, to study Art at the Herkomer School. Classified as unfit for military service, he also served as a Special Constable. In a surviving letter (now preserved in Bushey Museum), sent in May 1916, Lord Clarendon asked him to gather together vehicles to transport fifty German prisoners from Hatfield to unspecified land in West Hertfordshire, where they would work for the Board of Agriculture. The Board would supply the petrol.

Chewett also painted *Firelight* (see opposite) in 1915 for an exhibition to raise money for the Red Cross. Chewett lived in Bushey until his death in 1965, and the painting is still on display in his house.

In 1916, the Government began to issue War Bonds as a way of raising money and local savings associations were set up across the country. The Rickmansworth and Chorleywood War Savings Association, with Albert Freeman as Hon Treasurer, was founded in 1917. Companies and places of work were also involved, for instance National War Savings and War Certificates were sold to employees of John Dickinson and Co. The company introduced slogans into their works, such as 'Save money for England and Yourselves', as incentives to increase funding for the war effort. Dickinson and Co. also gave donations to the Red Cross.

The autumn of 1917 saw the introduction of a brand new weapon, the 'tank', at the Battle of Cambrai. Hoping to capitalize on the public

Firelight, *by Albert
Ranney Chewett.*
(Courtesy of the
Bushey Museum and
Art Gallery)

*War Bond Poster, issued
by the Parliamentary
War Savings Committee,
1915.*

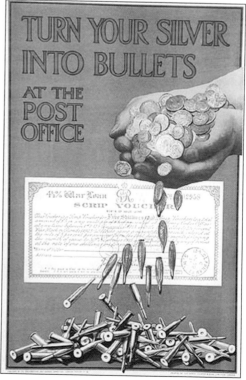

fascination with this phenomenon of modern warfare, it was decided to use a tank to help sell War Bonds and War Saving Certificates. On 26 November, a battle-scarred mark IV Tank, No. 141 'Egbert', was brought over from France and put on display in Trafalgar Square. The campaign was soon extended to the whole of the country, with six Tank Banks spending a week in each town or city.

The tank would arrive accompanied by soldiers, artillery guns and sometimes an aeroplane dropping pamphlets exhorting the people to invest in War Bonds, and put on a show for the crowds in order to demonstrate its capabilities. Civic dignitaries and local celebrities would add their prestige to the occasion, with speeches often made from on top of the tank, while two ladies sold War Bonds from a table set up inside. Each town or city visited would have a fundraising target and the amount raised would be reported in the papers. As an incentive, the town or city that invested the most per capita would win 'Egbert'. The eventual winner of the competition was West Hartlepool.

Tank 113 'Julian' visited Watford in May 1918, aided by singers, three local bands and two planes doing aerobatics overhead. It stayed in the market place attracting large crowds each evening for four days. Speeches of encouragement were made and £162,020 in War Bonds and Certificates was raised. The total nationwide investment in Tank Banks was over £2 million. 'Julian' was given to Aberdeen at the end of the War and remained there until 1940, when it was taken for scrap.

Schools were seen as fertile ground for pushing the desirability of thrift and investment in War Savings Certificates, and even the poorest areas often made significant contributions. On 8 May a teacher from Callow Land Boys CC, Watford, paraded forty-one of his boys triumphantly into town and bought forty-six certificates. By the end of the war, schools in Hemel Hempstead had raised £1,217 17s 0d.

There were many other forms of collection in aid of the war effort aside from requests for financial donations. In August 1917 Hertfordshire County War Agricultural Committee hoped to supply 'surprise packets for Fritz', in the form of conkers made into high explosives. With the aid of schoolboys, but also landowners, householders and farmers, they hoped to collect 250,000 tons of chestnuts per year, the spirit extract of a ton being the equivalent of 10cwt of barley.

Charities

Within a fortnight of the declaration of war, Lady Essex was making appeals on behalf of soldiers and sailors families, and by the last week of August 1914 the *Watford Illustrated* was already reporting on a number of fundraising events. On 22 August a practice match by the Watford Football Club had been played with the proceeds going to the War Relief Fund, a concert had been held at Kingham Hall on 26 August for the Prince of Wales Relief Fund, and on Sunday, 30 August Dickinson's Apsley Band and Vocalists had given another concert in the Park for the War Fund.

The Watford War Assistance Committee was set up on 10 August 1914. They co-ordinated and raised money for a number of causes: Belgian refugee relief; a women's unemployment committee; an infants' milk fund; the welfare of physically disabled soldiers, giving the veterans help and advice and trying to place them in suitable employment or training; money for the Prince of Wales Fund and their own General Fund.

The General Fund gave money to the Red Cross, to the District Hospital, to the YMCA, Soldiers' Homes and the Allies Flag Days. They also gave individual aid to people impoverished by the War through loss of earnings or because family breadwinners were serving. In the first sixteen months, of the 13,385 visits to homes 1,132 were to those of workers engaged in civil occupations, and 12,203 to the homes of soldiers and sailors, showing the greater proportion of aid supplied to those with family members in the forces.

The breakdown of funds raised for charities, as listed in the Watford War Assistance Committee Report of 1921 for August 1914 to December 1915, (rounded up) was:

Women's Employment	*£133*
Prince of Wales Fund	*£512*
Belgian Destitute Fund	*£289*
Watford War Assistance Fund	*£3,394*
Additional Donations	*£1,304*
Total	**£7,000**

Smaller funds were also set up in the surrounding area. The Bushey Local Fund Committee was made up of members of the Urban District

Council, local clergy and doctors. In Bushey 'gentlemen' and 'ladies' sat on the committees together, while in Chorleywood, for instance, they formed two separate committees.

As Christmas approached in 1914, families' thoughts were naturally with their loved ones serving abroad. The *Watford Observer* launched a 'Tobacco for the Troops' campaign to make sure the troops could enjoy a Christmas smoke, and there was even a Christmas Pudding Fund for servicemen. The Boy Scouts, who were involved in a number of activities, organized their own entertainment to raise funds for tobacco for the troops. Watford raised £325,000 for a war loan and came seventh in the country in raising money for Red Cross Day. Meanwhile, the Bushey War Relief Fund had already raised £1,000.

Fundraising efforts were not confined to British charities alone, for instance money was collected for Lord Robert's Indian Relief Fund and in 1915 a concert was held in aid of the French Red Cross in Bentley Priory, Bushey, for which Lucy Kemp-Welch designed the programme. In February 1916, Mrs Hankin Hardy, a Wesleyan nurse, who had served on the Eastern Front in Serbia from December 1914 to April 1915, reportedly 'gave an interesting account of her experiences' in Queen's Road Wesleyan Church. A collection was taken for the Serbian Relief Fund and the Queen's Road Soldiers' Home. In March 1918 the girls of Miss Turney's School, 'The Laurels' in George Street, Hemel Hempstead, put on 'An Entertainment', consisting of musical and dramatic performances at St Mary's Hall to raise money for the wounded soldiers recovering at the West Herts Hospital, Hemel Hempstead.

Fundraising concerts and events (a number used the sale of cards to raise money) continued throughout the War, but the priorities changed as the hardships increased on the Home Front and the wounded began returning home. The Ministry of Food Control was set up in 1916 and apart from introducing subsidised bread (the ninepenny loaf) it set up local food committees to organise voluntary rationing. The aim was not only to economize on food and fuel but also to provide cheap and nutritious meals. The first official communal kitchen in the area was set up in Bushey Heath in June 1917 and following its success two others were opened. Janet Murphey, in her book *Bushey During the Great War,* supplies the following menu:

Sample Ministry of Food Kitchen Menu	
Housewife soup	*1d*
Boiled beef and onions	*3 1/2d*
Cornish pasties	*2d*
Faggots	*1 1/2d each*
Fig pudding	*1d*
Syrup and semolina	*1d*
Rhubarb and sage mould	*1d*

The Watford War Assistance Committee ran a national kitchen in the Old Red Lion Elementary School in 1918, which was patronized by all classes, but particularly the middle classes. The dining room was free to customers who provided their own utensils. The following menu comes from the Watford War Assistance Committee's records:

Sample Watford War Assistance Committee Kitchen Menu	
Soup	*3d a pint*
Meat Pudding	*4d*
Fish Cakes	*3d*
Butter Beans	*2d per portion*
Potatoes	*1d*
Milk Pudding	*2d*
Custard Tart	*2d*

There was also a community kitchen at Watford, to which local firms contributed £300 each, which offered free food to soldiers and sailors, and a kitchen at Beechen Grove School selling cheap meals and takeaways to help working women.

Despite the introduction of rationing, food parcels were consistently sent to British prisoners behind enemy lines. These included civilians interned at the outbreak of war and held at Ruhleben internment camp. The *Watford News* reported in April 1918 that returning prisoners attested that they had been kept alive by the food sent out, which

To be filled up by Food Office before Issue.	Holder's Surname		KEEP THIS CARD CAREFULLY	RATIONING ORDER, 1918. N. 86.
	Christian Name			Food Office of Issue.
	Address			

To register for MEAT, BUTTER and SUGAR, fill up the counterfoils A, B and C on lower half of card, and give them to any Retailers you choose. The Retailers must write or stamp their names and addresses on these spaces. You will not be able to change your Retailer again without consent of the Food Office.	Name and Address of BUTCHER **A**	Name and Address of Retailer for............**D**
	Name and Address of BUTTER Retailer **B**	Name and Address of Retailer for............**E**
	Name and Address of SUGAR Retailer **C**	Name and Address of Retailer for............**F**

SPARE. Signature and Address of Holder.   Name and Address of Retailer for............ **D**

D

Keep this counterfoil and the top portion of the card, and read the accompanying leaflet of Instructions.

Ration card dated 1918.

proved that, despite the grumbles, the rationing system had worked, keeping everyone fed, civilians, sailors and soldiers alike.

As a result of the German advance through Belgium, a host of desperate refugees fled across the Channel. In September 1914 the British Government offered these 'victims of war the hospitality of the British nation' and towns across Hertfordshire took them in. Totalling over a quarter of a million people it was the largest refugee movement in British history. Many of the Belgians were said to have lost everything and there was an immediate outburst of public sympathy for their plight.

The *Watford Illustrated* appealed on their behalf:

*The Belgians who have had to flee their country are deserving
of all the aid we can give them, they have stood the first
impetuous rush of the Germans, and nobly have their soldiers
stood their ground and delayed them.*

On 29 August 1914, both the *Watford Illustrated* and *Watford Observer*
reported on the collection of clothing and household linens for Belgian
soldiers and civilians suffering as a consequence of the war. These
donations were sent on to Monsieur Navaun of the Belgian Legation.
Mrs Olive Thomas organized a committee of ladies and launched an
appeal for the refugees, combined with another appeal for the comforts
of the soldiers. She initiated an 'excellent scheme' for a 'Home of Rest
for thirty Belgian women and children of the better class'. Eight
shillings a week would support an adult and 5 shillings a child. The
first refugees arrived at the beginning of September.

On 5 September, the Bushey Committee for the Relief of Destitute
Belgians was formed. Mr George Jaggard, a local builder, donated his
twenty-room house, 'Elmcote', in Aldenham Road, which was capable

'Hillendale', Bushey Heath, once a home for Belgian refugees.

of accommodating up to thirty women and children. The *Watford Illustrated* reported a week later that twenty-three refugees had arrived from Liège and the house was renamed locally as 'Liège House'. In October, Hillendale (now Powis Court) in the Rutts was also opened to the refugees. A lecture about Belgium was put on at the Parish Hall in Falconer Road and £13 raised for the refugee fund.

Funds were raised by public appeal by the Watford War Assistance Committee for Belgian refugee relief. Between August 1914 and December 1915, the Committee estimated that a hundred refugees cost £470 per day to house and clothe; houses were offered for free, electricity was supplied and gas provided gratis; bedding and furniture were lent by local residents. In addition, gifts were given to the refugees by local people and a Hospitality Committee undertook their supervision and gave the refugees advice. Seven houses were occupied by the refugees in Watford, with another two in Bushey and two more in Rickmansworth.

Refugees were also housed at Hunton Bridge, Abbots Langley, Kings Langley and Chorleywood. The Committee in St Andrews Ward took one Watford house and then raised funds and maintained a number of Belgians at its own charge. Refugees were similarly looked after in Rickmansworth, while in Watford, 210 Belgians passed through the register, seventy-five at a time. By 1919 there were still thirty-five Belgians remaining in the local area and they were given money to help them repatriate.

For the girls of Abbots Hill School, near Hemel Hempstead, the holidays meant knitting comforts for soldiers, while their parents organized entertainments for the wives and children of servicemen. Some of them also took in Belgian refugees, both individuals and families. Abbots Hill itself adopted a Belgian family and put them up in a house it rented in Kings Langley. The school looked after the family, furnishing the house and supplying food, until they suddenly departed in May 1915.

Local churches were active in their own way, organizing parade services for the troops and concerts for their entertainment while their parishioners sent comforts and parcels to the soldiers. At Beechen Grove Baptist Church every effort was made to keep in contact with the hundred male members of the congregation who were now serving. The *Watford Illustrated* (12 Sept 1914) reported that the Rev C.B. McCullagh, BA, of the Wesleyan Church, Queen's Road had organized a correspondence circle to keep in contact with the soldiers from his church.

But his church was not only concerned with its own congregation, for as soon as the troops arrived in Watford, they set up a Soldiers' Home in the Old School Room and transformed it into 'the best Soldiers' Home in the town'. Local people were asked to provide a bathroom for the soldiers by a man dubbed the 'Commander of the Bath Department'. Mr Mobbs managed to provide 500 free baths a week. One house took in twelve soldiers a week. The number of baths was soon increased to 1,100 and they also set up a Postal Department; 47,310 letters were posted in the box on the table, using stationary provided by Dickinson & Co.

War Hospital Supply Depots

The War created an urgent need for medical supplies, bandages and emergency clothing. Within the first three weeks, the *Watford Observer* (22 August 1914) carried an appeal for 1,000 padded splints. To meet the demand for nightshirts, gowns and bed-jackets for soldiers in hospital, garments were made by hand by groups and individuals both at home and abroad, often paying for the materials out of their own pockets.

Initially the work was largely unregulated, but in 1915 The Central Work Rooms at Burlington House, Piccadilly, London, began the job of coordinating willing women across the country by establishing local Work Parties, where they could contribute their time and skills. This resulted in more than 2,700 War Hospital Supply Depots and Work Parties being organized by private individuals throughout the United Kingdom and overseas, and the contribution made by these groups became essential to maintaining the supply of dressings and garments to many hospitals. Each individual who registered a work party gave an address, often of their private residence.

In Watford and close by there were nine Depots. They were run by:

J. Harrison, Esq., 'Lyndhurst'
Miss F.M. Plumb, 66 Marlborough Road
Miss M.A. Rogers, 18 Salters Terrace, (where the women of St Andrews Church turned their hand to whatever came along, including organizing splint working parties.)

Miss A. Pitkin, 24 Aldenham Road, Oxhey
Mrs D.E.R. Morgan, Letchmore House
Mrs Baker, New House Farm, Garston
Miss J.E.F. Sayle, Bushey Cottage, New Bushey
Miss Mildred Hodgson, 'The Limes'
Miss E. Reading, 17 Queen's Road

There were two Depots in Bushey, run by: Mrs Crawhall-Wilson, at 12 Grange Road and Mrs C. Roberts, at 'Noyna', Avenue Rise. The Hon Mrs Capell, Countess of Essex, ran five Depots in Chorleywood, while Mrs Hedingham ran a Depot at 'Farleigh', Dickinson Avenue in nearby Croxley Green.

In Hemel Hempstead there were two Depots, one run by Mrs Hubert Secretan of Bennetts End and the other by the Hon Mrs Susan Talbot, of Marchmont House, the wife of Gustavus Talbot, Mayor of Hemel Hempstead (and MP from 1918). She had lost her youngest son, Lieutenant Humfrey Richard Talbot of the 3rd Prince of Wales' Dragoon Guards on 13 November 1914. He had served in the Indian Army before going to France on 30 October. His trench was hit by shellfire near Ypres and despite being wounded himself he tended to his men. He died of his wounds, aged twenty-five, and was buried in Ypres town cemetery.

At Kings Langley Depots were run by Mrs W. Archer of Langley Rise and Mrs Shaw of Langleybury Vicarage, while in Abbots Langley Lady Gladys Kindersley ran a Depot at Langley House. Her husband, Robert Molesworth Kindersley (KBE), later 1st Baron Kindersley, was a Governor of the Hudson Bay Company and a director of the Bank of England. She had six children, the eldest, Lionel, was killed in the war and Hugh served in the Scots Guards and was awarded the Military Cross in 1918 aged just nineteen. Lady Kindersley was also the local secretary of the Prisoner of War Fund.

The large houses of the Rickmansworth area also played their part. Lady Ebury, Emilie, wife of Robert Wellesley Grosvenor, and friend of American artists, the writer Henry James, the influential photographer Alvin Langdon Coburn (1882–1966) and the painter Leon Dabo (1864–1960), used her stately home at Moor Park. Mrs Stewart ran a Depot nearby at Batchworth House and Susan Harris, Countess of Malmesbury, the widowed second wife of James Howard Harris, 3rd Earl of Malmesbury used Lockwell House.

At St Albans, there was Mrs Hugh Anson, at Sandridge Vicarage and Mrs Drake at Batch Wood. Along the way into London there were:

Mrs Beatty Smyth of 'The Beeches' in Shenley
Miss S. Wylde, at 'Oakbank' and Mrs J. B. Arnot, at 'Tigh-Na-Duin' in Radlett, Mrs Everett, Mrs Reginald Brayans at 'Elm Croft', and Mrs John Terry at 'Manaton' in Elstree
Miss K. E. Jameson at 'Elladene' in Borehamwood

In Barnet Mrs Weber ran the B.W.H. Supply Depot, 40 High Street, supported by Mrs Duncan in Hadley Common and Mrs Henry Trotter at Christ Church Vicarage.

CHAPTER 3

Casualties and Veterans

The Voluntary Aid Detachments

Since 1909 Voluntary Aid Detachments (VADs) had been established as part of the Territorial organization in England and Wales. They were attached variously to the British Red Cross Society, the Order of St John or the Territorial Forces Association. As with the Territorial Force, the Detachments were intended for home defence only, but in the event both served abroad in France, Belgium, Gallipoli and Mesopotamia.

In 1914 the majority of their members were women, most men having been called up for military service. Women's Detachments were smaller than the men's, with one Commandant (either male or female), a Lady Superintendent (preferably a trained nurse) and twenty women (four of whom had to be trained cooks). Male Detachments comprised a Commandant, a medical officer, a quartermaster, a pharmacist, four section leaders and forty-eight men.

The role of individual nurses, who became known as VADs, was mainly supportive. They acted as nursing assistants, working alongside qualified nurses. They were trained by the British Red Cross in first aid and how to make beds, fed patients, give blanket baths, and keep a ward clean. The rules of their constitution were flexible, so they also undertook a variety of other jobs, as general cleaners, cooks, ambulance drivers and administrators, as need demanded. At the outbreak of war, some 46,000 women were serving in Voluntary Aid Detachments. By the end of the conflict, over 90,000 had registered. In the first week of the war, Watford's local VAD had fifty ladies hard at work in St John's Hall making uniforms. The Countess of Essex offered Cassiobury House to the Detachment for a hospital, but it was not taken up.

Strafe the Tailor—A Bad Fit of the "Blues."

Postcard by R. Stoddart, 1916.

Hospitals

By late 1914, once casualties began streaming back from the Front, it soon became clear that the existing hospital and post-trauma care facilities were not adequate. Institutions and large country houses within the county were soon being converted into military hospitals. Digwell House in Welwyn became a home for wounded Australian officers, Ashridge House a hospital and Napsbury Hospital a military hospital. Private houses and buildings were also lent for the duration of the War.

The wounded inmates were issued with a blue hospital uniform which, judging by the 1916 postcard illustrated by R. Stoddart, did not always come up to expectations. *The Times* (20 October 1916) announced that a Mr Randell was to:

> *ask the Secretary of State for War on Tuesday whether he is aware that the blue uniform supplied to the wounded soldiers seems to be defective, in the outer skin of the garment, which is of flannelette, when washed shrinks at a rate from the lining, and that this problem produces an unsightly and bad-fitting garment; and whether flannel clothes cannot be given to the wounded instead.*

Hemel Hempstead:

The West Herts (Voluntary) Hospital, which relied on charitable donations, was originally established in a row of converted cottages at Piccotts End in 1827. It served a large area from Bushey to Tring, including St Albans and Harpenden. Larger premises were built, which became known as Cheere House, in 1832. In 1877 Princess Mary of Teck opened new hospital buildings with room for fifty patients and seven nurses, and Cheere House was let to The King's College Hospital Convalescent Home in 1878. In 1899 the hospital installed X-ray facilities, claiming to be amongst the first in England to do so. From 1890, nurses were able to train on the premises and in 1919 its function as a general nursing training school was approved.

Early in the war, the Hospital offered the British Red Cross the use of twenty beds for soldiers by converting the Outpatients' Waiting Hall into a twelve-bed ward and adding seven beds in the Astley Cooper Ward and another bed in the Fisher Balcony. In 1917 an appeal raised £2,000 for a new temporary ward, the Windsor Ward, with the addition of another thirty-five beds. Over 800 soldiers passed through the hospital and after the War it was allocated for disabled servicemen. King's College handed over Cheere House to the Hertfordshire Red Cross Society for up to forty soldiers, while Boxmoor House, a private house owned by Mrs and Miss Bouwens, became a VAD Hospital providing twenty beds.

Postcard of Boxmoor House in Hemel Hempstead, which was used as a VAD hospital in the War.

In nearby Gadebridge, Gadebridge Hospital was a specialist venereal disease hospital for 800 men. A former artillery training camp, it was taken over in July 1917. It was converted to a 350-bed officers' hospital after the war. Shafford Camp, near St Albans, also included huts for a 106-bed specialist venereal disease unit.

Napsbury:

In September 1915 the Middlesex County Asylum, Napsbury, near London Colney, with a total of around 1600 beds, was put under War Office management, initially for soldiers suffering from shellshock but, on 14 May 1916, it became the County of Middlesex War Hospital for the accommodation of sick and wounded soldiers. This change meant that the mentally ill patients had to be re-located into other institutions nearby.

The hospital included a specialist military psychiatric unit with capacity for 250 men, although during a debate in the House of Commons in May 1915 it was said there were 320 soldiers suffering from shell shock in one block at the hospital. The number of these cases is usually put at 350 men, all described certifiable as 'nerve-shaken'. They were treated by the Army Medical Service, not by the asylum administration, and kept absolutely apart from the certified civilian

Postcard of Napsbury Hospital.

patients. If the military patients proved to be incurable, then they might be sent on to public asylums.

In his book on the experiences of ordinary soldiers suffering from mental illness during the War (*Forgotten Lunatics of the Great War*), Peter Barham cites Napsbury as an example of a more enlightened hospital regime, where all soldiers were treated equally. The sheer number of casualties and the increasingly vocal civilian response put pressure on mental health experts to treat shell shock in a more egalitarian manner than previously. Class prejudices had meant that officers were treated more sympathetically in many hospitals, but Napsbury was in the forefront of the New Psychology. By giving credence to the stories of the ordinary soldier, they allowed him to apply the label of shell shock to his condition as a way of coming to terms with any sense of failure or accusations of unmanly conduct. The average stay at the hospital for shell shock victims was five months, before they either returned to duty or were sent home.

The war poet and composer Ivor Gurney, who was gassed at St Julien and suffered a mental collapse while recovering in County Durham, was transferred to Napsbury in July 1917. He remained there until his discharge from the army in October 1918, with a pension of 12 shillings per week. Tragically, Gurney never really recovered his mental or physical health and he died of tuberculosis in 1937.

Ivor Gurney wrote the following lines while at Napsbury:

> *...The bell of grief and lost delight.*
> *Gay leaves slow fluttered to the ground.*
>
> *Sudden, that sense of peace and prayer*
> *Like vapour faded. Round the bend*
> *Swung lines of khaki without end...*
> *Common was water, earth and air;*
> *Death seemed a hard thing not to mend.*
> (From *Toussaints*, September 1918.)

The name of Gurney's poem, 'Toussaints', refers to 'All Saints Day', an important festival of commemoration in France and the poem makes mention of Merville, near Ypres where there is a large war cemetery.

Entertainments were laid on for the troops at Napsbury, including cinema shows, and theatrical and musical performances and, once able, some patients were retained by the hospital to work in the wards,

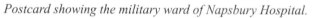

Postcard showing the military ward of Napsbury Hospital.

kitchen and workshops. In 1918 the hospital was renamed Napsbury Mental Hospital and returned to its original purpose. The site closed in 1998 and has since been redeveloped for residential purposes.

St Albans VAD Hospital:

In December 1914, Bricket House in St Albans, a large mansion rented from the Rev. P. Deedes, was taken over by the War Office for use as a field hospital. It was run by the St Albans branch of the British Red Cross Society and, in March 1915, it became the St Albans VAD Hospital, an auxiliary military hospital with thirty-five beds for sick and wounded soldiers. It was affiliated to the Napsbury War Hospital and run by Mrs L. Boycott, of Gompards House, St Albans, who was responsible for the nursing and household staff, drawn from the Herts/38 VAD. By 1917 the Hospital had forty beds. It closed in 1918, but during its operational lifetime, some 2,298 patients received treatment there.

After the War, the Demobilisation Committee of the Hertfordshire Branch of the British Red Cross Society sold off their equipment for £777 8s 6d. However, the work of the VAD was not yet done, as the Branch pioneered the opening of orthopaedic clinics to provide continuing physiotherapy for ex-servicemen. The first Orthopaedic Clinic opened in the stables of Bricket House, with the Herts/38 in attendance and doing clerical work. At first, on-going care for discharged servicemen was provided, then later massage and electrical treatments for physically disabled persons and children. The Clinic closed in 1948 with the advent of the NHS.

The Cottage Hospital in Watford:

From 1915 to 1916, according to *Kelly's Directory*, the hospital contained eighty beds, six cots and was fitted with X-ray equipment. This proved inadequate for the number of wounded, and local Voluntary Aid Detachment units were set up in alternative buildings made available by local residents and the Council.

Watford Isolation Hospital:

This hospital for the treatment of contagious diseases was situated in Tolpits Lane, West Watford. Due to the presence of troops billeted in Watford and the surrounding areas, there was a rise in the number of cases admitted, especially of measles and German measles. A decrease in cases in 1916, following a lull in military activity, allowed the places in which troops were billeted to be properly disinfected.

In 1918 there was a devastating outbreak of influenza, known as Spanish Flu, which affected an estimated 500 million people across the world. The effects were so deadly that an advisory poster was produced and displayed around the town telling people how to protect themselves during the epidemic. Thirty cases were admitted to the hospital, of which eleven died. A notable casualty of the epidemic was Leefe Robinson who had downed the SL-11 airship. He died, aged twenty-three, on 31 December 1918 and is buried at Harrow Weald, Stanmore, just over the border in Middlesex.

Lady's Close Auxiliary (VAD) Hospital:
A private house in Watford, Lady's Close, was used as an auxiliary hospital. Today it is a Grade II listed building and part of Watford Girl's Grammar School.

The site of the hospital is commemorated by a plaque:

> *The British Red Cross Society and the Order of Saint John gratefully acknowledge that this building was converted and used as an auxiliary hospital worked by a voluntary staff during the Great War.*

The Wall Hall VAD Hospital:

Wall Hall Hospital in Aldenham opened in June 1916, with twenty-four beds. It was housed in a large garage lent by John Pierpoint (Jack) Morgan Jr, the son of the founder of the American banking dynasty JP Morgan, who had bought the Hall in 1910. He also generously provided a great part of the equipment for the Hospital. Originally intended as a convalescent home for typhoid patients it proved unsatisfactory and was then used for convalescents recovering from other illnesses and wounds. The Hospital closed in February 1919. A Red Cross Plaque commemorates its service during the War.

Glen Almond Convalescent Home:

A convalescent home for Australian Nurses was situated in King Henry's Lane, St Albans. In July 1916, the shipping magnate Mr.

Harold C.C. McIlwraith, a Director of the White Star Line, lent his country home for the duration to the Commonwealth (Australian) Government and the Australian Imperial Forces for use as a convalescent home for Sisters and Nurses of the Australian Army Nursing Service (AANS). A Sister of the AANS was placed in charge.

Chorleywood Pavilion Auxiliary Hospital:
This Hospital took over the premises of Lady Ela Russell's former Drill Hall on the Chorleywood House Estate, Rickmansworth Road. The hall became an auxiliary (convalescent) military hospital. A contemporary photograph in *Chorleywood, Chenies, Loudwater & Heronsgate: a social history* (2008), by Ian Foster, shows some eighteen patients, with four members of the nursing staff posed outside the hall.

Barnet War Hospital:
The Barnet Union Workhouse, situated on part of Barnet Common on the south side of Wellhouse Lane, opened in 1838 with accommodation for about 200 inmates. An infirmary block was built in 1886 to the east of the workhouse, and another one was added to the south in 1901. In 1915 Pickering Lodge, a mansion adjacent to the workhouse, was acquired for use as a nurses' home for the infirmary, complete with an ornamental garden and a tennis lawn.

Despite the uncertainties of wartime, the Barnet Guardians had begun to build a new infirmary early in 1915. When the work had to be postponed due to labour shortages, the Army Council took over the project and completed the infirmary in June 1916, and it became the Barnet War Hospital. Between 1916 and 1918 some 6,000 wounded and sick soldiers were treated at the Hospital. In October 1919 the infirmary was handed back to the Guardians, who were able to purchase all the equipment from the War Office for 10 per cent less than it had cost in 1915. The Guardians renamed it the Wellhouse Hospital, after the ancient well reputed to contain physic qualities; Samuel Pepys had once taken these waters. Today, the hospital is part of the Barnet and Chase Farm Hospitals NHS Trust.

High Barnet VAD Hospital:
The Deacons of the Barnet United Reformed Church lent their church hall, built in 1909, to the War Office for use as an auxiliary military

(convalescent) hospital. Ewen Hall in Wood Street, Barnet, was converted in March 1915, with an initial capacity of twenty-five beds. It was run by the Hertford/32 Voluntary Aid Department and affiliated to Edmonton Military Hospital. The Commandant, Miss Winifred Game, was also in charge of Ken Cottage Auxiliary Hospital in Hadley Wood.

By 1917 it had forty beds, later increased to fifty-two and by September 1918 there were seventy beds. It closed in April 1919. In July 1920 a framed certificate was presented to the Church by the Army Council as a record of thanks for the use of the Hall as a VAD Hospital, signed by the Secretary of State for War, Winston Churchill.

Ken Cottage Auxiliary Hospital:
No. 4 Crescent West, Hadley Wood was used as a convalescent home for wounded servicemen. The house was lent by Mr. R.F. Sandon who lived next door in No. 5, known as 'Ken Cottage'. Opened in March 1915, it had ten beds and was staffed by the Hertford/32 Voluntary Aid Detachment, which had been established in the district before 1914 under the charge of a trained nursing sister. All cleaning, cooking and catering was undertaken by local women from Hadley Wood. The hospital's wartime career is commemorated by a standard Red Cross Plaque on the wall of the house, now renumbered No. 34.

Hillside Auxiliary Hospital:
In April 1915, the British Red Cross Society was given 'Hillside' in Barnet Road, Potters Bar, rent-free for use as an auxiliary hospital. Lady Rachel Byng's Convalescent Home for Wounded Soldiers moved there from The Mount, Hadley (near Barnet). By 1917 Lady Byng had acquired The Mount from Lady Muriel Willoughby and the hospital returned there on 20 May. In the following month 'Hillside' was put up for sale but, as it had remained unsold by March 1918, it was used to house prisoners of war working on local farms.

Potters Bar VAD Hospital:
The Potters Bar Hospital opened in 1914 in Little Heath Wood House, a large country mansion in Hawkshead Road, Potters Bar. The owner of the house, Mrs. McDowell Nathan, also provided milk and garden produce for the staff and patients. The Hospital had eighteen beds and

was run by the local VAD. It was well supported locally by subscriptions and weekly pound days.

Rickmansworth VAD Hospital

This hospital was located in two separate buildings, St Augustine's Hall, Park Road and The Studio, Rectory Lane, and was managed by the local VAD. St Augustine's Hall, with twenty beds, was a former malthouse. Lent by Father J. Julien, the building had been bought by the Augustinians of the Assumption. At The Studio there were sixteen beds. This site, provided by Mr E. Beckett, was a house with a large lofty room.

The first patients to the Hospital were wounded Belgian soldiers, transferred from The Royal Naval Hospital Haslar (no longer a military hospital) in Gosport, Hampshire. In March 1915, the Hospital was affiliated to the First Eastern General Hospital, in Cambridge, a military hospital established by the Royal Army Medical Corps, and was fully occupied. By 1917 the Hospital increased its capacity to forty-two beds and had changed its affiliation to the Napsbury Hospital. It closed in 1918 and eventually The Studio became a dance studio.

The Institute, Croxley Green

The Institute was a VAD hospital under the patronage of J. Dickinson & Co. It contained thirty-five beds. On 5 September 1917 the *Harrowgate Herald* carried the following story of Sergeant Bagenal, a patient at Croxley Green.

> *Sergeant H Bagenal, RAMC, son of Mr P H Bagenal, Local Government Board Officer, has received the Distinguished Conduct Medal for conspicuous gallantry on the field of battle at Bernafay Wood, on the Somme, in July, 1916. He had been in charge of stretcher-bearers for 48 hours under shellfire, and had carried a message under barrage to another dressing station. The gallant sergeant had been severely wounded, and the medal was presented to him by General Mackenzie at Croxley Green VAD Hospital.*

Underfield, Borehamwood:

In Borehamwood, Mrs Jarvin Dickson also gave over 'Underhill', her private house with a capacity for eight beds, as a hospital during the War.

CHAPTER 4

The War Dead

During the conflict, the press often provided the first line of communication with the battlefield, and it played the most prominent role in commemorating the fallen. The first known Watford fatality of the Great War was Sergeant Thomas Michael Horgan of the 2nd Battalion Royal Inniskilling Fusiliers. He was reported as 'killed in action in France', by the *Watford Illustrated* on 19 September 1914.

Bereaved relatives received a personal letter of condolence from the King, usually addressed to the soldier's mother: 'I join with my grateful people in sending you this memorial of a brave life given for others in the Great War.' Commemoration for the fallen did not begin in earnest until after the War was over, and often relatives did not know the exact circumstances of their loved one's death.

Public Commemoration

Initially, the dead were buried in the nearest cemeteries with little documentation. Sir Fabian Ware, a director of the Rio Tinto Mining Company and too old to fight, was commanding a mobile unit of the British Red Cross in France when he decided to use his position to bring order to the chaos of military burials. His work eventually received official sanction and the Imperial War Graves Commission was founded in 1917.

After the War, the matter of how to commemorate the dead became a pressing and controversial issue. At first, those who could afford it, usually the relatives of officers, acted privately to retrieve the bodies of their loved ones from the battlefields for burial. This private care of the dead was perceived as a right by relatives, but it was challenged successfully by Ware, who saw the exercise as one of class privilege. Instead he championed the collective commemoration of the dead, on or near the battlefield where they had fallen. He argued that if men of all classes had been asked to sacrifice themselves for the New Army, then men of all classes should be remembered together in death.

> *The point of view that seems to me to be often overlooked in this matter is that of the officers themselves, who in ninety-nine cases out of a hundred will tell you that if they are killed* [they] *would wish to be among their men.*

Controversial at the time, this form of collective remembrance has become an accepted part of our heritage. In November 1918, Sir Frederic Kenyon, the director of the British Museum, headed a committee for the Commission charged with how to deal with the new situation. In his report he described his vision for the war cemeteries within which:

> *at some prominent spot will rise the Cross, as the symbol of the Christian faith and of the self-sacrifice of the men who now lie beneath its shadow.*

Despite the overriding Christian symbolism, the Commission believed in honouring all casualties equally, without distinction on account of rank, race or creed and the architects were free to interpret this vision with their own ideas. Thus individual cemeteries developed their own character, while more or less conforming to the same pattern. In any cemetery with over forty graves, there would be the Cross of Sacrifice, designed by the architect Sir Reginald Blomfield, to represent the faith of the majority.

By using a simple cross, embedded with a bronze sword and mounted on an octagonal base, Blomfield hoped, in his words, 'to keep clear of any of the sentimentalities of Gothic'. Cemeteries with over 1,000 burials had a Stone of Remembrance, designed by Sir Edwin Lutyens to commemorate those of all faiths and none. He based the geometry of the structure on studies of the Parthenon, again creating a neutral form, rather than include associations with particular religions.

'A corner of a foreign field forever England'

A typical example of the commemoration on the gravestone of a local fallen soldier at the Merville Communal Cemetery, France reads:

10881 Private William Allen, 2nd Bn. Royal Fusiliers, 13/04/1918, aged 37. Husband of Harriet Allen, of 33, Clay Hill, Bushey, Herts, father of James, Helen, Anne, Emma and Albert. Plot I. E. 37.

Buried at Sea

Some servicemen could never be given a grave. Burial at sea is a naval practice and the navy commemorates its losses through its own specially designated memorials. The bodies of other soldiers were also lost on the battlefield. Two brothers from Bushey come under both of those categories: Able Seaman David George Perkins, RN, and Ebenezer Perkins were two of the five sons of George, a retired Metropolitan Police officer.

David Perkins, already a veteran of fourteen years in the Royal Navy, was aboard HMS *Swiftsure* as part of the fleet sent to support the Gallipoli landings. David suffered gas poisoning and died of wounds on 6 June 1915, at the age of thirty-three. He was buried at sea and is remembered on the Chatham Naval Memorial in Kent. Ebenezer was killed at St Quentin on 23 March 1918, aged twenty, and is remembered on the Arras Memorial, France.

Local War Memorials

The public at home needed a focus for remembrance and their own visible memorials to the dead to counterbalance the mass graves and monuments on foreign soil, such as the Thiepval Memorial to the Missing of the Somme designed by Lutyens. To satisfy this need the most famous memorial, the Cenotaph, also by Lutyens, was built close to the tomb of the 'Unknown Warrior' in Westminster Abbey, as a national symbol of grief. This template was followed on a local level with stone-built town and parish cenotaphs, as well as company and school memorials, which brought together the names of those united by a common local heritage.

The sentiments expressed in quotations on the memorials emphasise notions of sacrifice, honour or duty. These often consist of Biblical

Radlett War Memorial.

references, typically, 'He saved others; himself He cannot save' (Matthew 27.42, King James Version), said of Jesus as he hung on the cross, or 'For God so loved the world, that He gave His only begotten Son, that whosoever believeth in Him should not perish, but have everlasting life' (John 3.16, KJV), which equate suffering with the Christian message of sacrifice from the Crucifixion.

The simple patriotic expression 'for King and Country' was also often used to encapsulate the notion of sacrifice with duty, while the quotation on the Radlett Memorial, 'Awake remembrance of these valiant dead' from *Henry V* (Act 1 Scene 2), evokes Shakespeare's most patriotic play to combine feelings of courage and honour with mourning.

Local commemoration was not immediate and, when instigated, it took a number of forms: rolls of honour, street memorials, church and cemetery memorials, and village and town war memorials. By the

Commemorative plaque outside former URC, Bushey.

1920s most places had some form or mixture of public commemorative display.

The smaller memorials, often sober or austere, can be easily passed by today. A discreet plaque on the front of the former United Reformed Church in the High Street, Bushey, does not allude to any modern feelings of doubt, which would have been too painful at the time, but states a belief in the justness of the cause, emphasising that the sacrifice made by the fallen had been worthwhile. For those who had lost a number of members of their family seeing their names together on the local war memorial may have been a source of comfort.

The three Andrews, and two Ashbys and Watsons, on the Bushey plaque (pictured above) are presumably brothers. The inscription on the plaque reads as follows:

*To the Glory of God and in Loving and Honoured Memory of
the Following Men Associated with this Church who Laid Down
their Lives in the Cause of Justice & Freedom in the Great War
1914–1919*

...

*He Saved Others
Himself He Could Not Save.*

The same names may appear in different locations, reflecting the
different aspects of people's lives, as parishioners, workers and, later,
soldiers. In Watford Central Library, the Roll of Honour records the
818 names of those killed in the Great War; a pattern repeated in towns
throughout the land.

Other public buildings, such as halls and hospitals, also preserved
their own memory of the War. Villages built halls for communal use
which could also act as a constant reminder. The Chorleywood War
Memorial Hall opened on 11 November 1922 and is situated on the
south-west side of the Common. It was funded by donations from local

people and public subscriptions, at a cost of £5,000. The construction, by the local family firm of Darvell (who donated the memorial board inside the hall), was based on the same plans as the village hall at Bovingdon.

While the hall gave a utilitarian focus, in Letchmore Heath individual houses bear their own more personal testimony, bringing the fallen eerily to mind as they strode out into the unknown. On the wall of a house opposite the Village Hall, is the inscription:

> *Harry Walton Keen left this house April 25 1917 to fight for his King and Country and fell in action in France April 18th 1918 aged 19.*

The village hall in Letchmore Heath bearing the legend, '1914 Aldenham + War + Memorial 1918', above the entrance.

Houses in Letchmore Heath with memorial plaques.

Not only did members of the same families go to war together, for instance the six Grange brothers from Bushey (who all survived), but whole bands of friends, clubs or streets. Those who survived wanted their own collective memorial to their comrades. A stone carved on a wall in Hollywell Hill, St Albans, listing the fallen among local neighbours, is one such example.

For their official war memorial smaller towns and villages often followed the template of a Celtic cross on a plinth or a simple tapering stone monolith on a plinth, which could be situated on the village green or in the parish churchyard. The Abbots Langley memorial in the churchyard of St Lawrence the Martyr, erected in 1920, however, follows Sir Reginald Blomfield's Cross of Sacrifice; a simple, large, white stone cross with an inlaid sword, on a plinth. It records the names of the ninety-three men from the parish who died either during the conflict, or as a result of wounds received.

Aldenham War Memorial, situated on the Village Green in Letchmore Heath, is in the form of a Celtic cross on a square section plinth, the whole mounted on a three-step base. The names of the fallen are inscribed on the two opposite faces of the cross. A similar memorial was erected in Elstree in 1921. A simple plain monolith, with the names of the thirty-nine killed or missing, the Borehamwood Memorial was erected in the same year.

Not all the war dead were killed on the battlefield. In local parish church cemeteries there are reminders that many suffered as casualties, only to die of their wounds on their return home. Buried in the churchyard in Abbot's Langley are three servicemen commemorated

Grave in St James Churchyard, Bushey, of G. Croucher, Royal Berkshire Regiment, who died on 5 February 1920, aged twenty-nine.

Commemorative Cross to the War Dead, St James's Parish Church, Bushey.

on the War Memorial, and Oliver Maitland, Rifleman 2072 of the Post Office Rifles, who died on British soil on 25 February 1915. There are three other servicemen who died in 1920, whose names are not on the War Memorial but who were probably war casualties. Similarly in St James, Bushey, there are two graves of servicemen who died of their wounds. One of them, G. Croucher of the Royal Berkshire Regiment, died at Netley Hospital, Southampton (further details below).

Major towns erected significant stone-built memorials situated in prominent locations. The St Albans war memorial, unveiled on 22 May 1921, in Peter's Street, follows the Celtic cross model but on a larger scale. The tall tapering cross is on an elaborate plinth. It records the names of the 634 local men, including fifty-seven officers up to the rank of Captain, who died in the war. Of these Lieutenant A.V. Smith had the distinction of holding the French Croix de Guerre and Private Edward Warner (mentioned in Chapter One) was awarded the Victoria Cross. Other medals awarded included five MCs, ten MMs, one DFC, one DCM, one MSM, and seven other men were mentioned in dispatches.

For memorials intended to make a more artistic statement there was no native precedent, so designers usually looked back to ancient Greece and Rome for inspiration. This type often included a sculptural element, with figures of the dying or wounded, and personifications of mourning or victory which used classical models as a starting point.

Watford War Memorials

As the largest town in the area, Watford has a number of memorials. The set of striking bronze figures situated outside the Town Hall acts as the focus of Remembrance Day services and is popularly taken to be the main town war memorial. However, Watford's official war memorial stands largely forgotten in Vicarage Road Cemetery, close to the entrance gate. Erected in 1929 by the Imperial War Graves Commission, it has the Cross of Sacrifice. On Sunday 28 February 1929, fifty-five servicemen were buried there and the memorial was unveiled by the Mayor, Alderman F.J.B. Hemming, in front of 1,000 people, with a dedication service following.

There is also a Celtic cross style memorial outside Christ Church, St Albans Road, and a memorial stone in Leavesden, which is believed to have formerly been situated on the doorway to the public reading rooms in the High Road. Christ Church is a daughter church of St

Andrews, on the other side of the railway line. Here there is also a street shrine to the First World War dead. The shrine bears the following inscription:

> *In a nearby street this shrine was used during the Great War to keep in prayerful remembrance those who died on active service. The wooden cross above marked for many years the last resting place of an unknown soldier. The cross and shrine are here preserved that future generations may never forget the sacrifice of those who died. 'These are they which come out of great tribulation and washed their robes and made them white in the blood of the Lamb. Therefore are they before the throne of God.*

Inscribed on the plinth of the cross of the memorial outside the Church are the names of the local men who died in the conflict.

The Grade II War Memorial outside Watford Town Hall consists of three bronze male figures on a white Portland stone base. The sculptures originally stood in front of the Peace Memorial Hospital. Mary Pownall Bromet, the artist who created the memorial, had made the statues in plaster during the War and offered the figures as a group to the Hospital in the 1920s. Money was raised by local subscription to cast them in bronze and they were unveiled by the Earl of Clarendon on 1 July 1928. The statues were later moved to their current location in 1971.

There are no individuals named on the memorial, but the central standing male nude with outstretched arm represents 'Victory', while the seated nude figure on the left bears the inscription 'To the Fallen', dated 1914, and the one to right 'To the Wounded', dated 1916.

Mary Pownall Bromet was one of Britain's leading sculptors during the early twentieth century, a President of the Society of Women Artists and an Associate Member of the Royal Society of British Sculptors. She was born near Leigh, Lancashire, in 1862, and from 1897 to 1900 she studied extensively abroad, in Frankfurt-am-Main, Rome and in Paris, where she came under the influence of Rodin. Back home, in 1902 she married Alfred Bromet, a barrister, and they moved to Lime Lodge in Pinner Road, Oxhey, where she had a studio. Her husband was a friend of Stanley Baldwin and the house was often used to host Conservative gatherings. Mary exhibited throughout Europe, at the

Mary Pownall Bromet's memorial outside Watford Town Hall.

Royal Academy and in provincial British galleries. A sculptor of great technical ability, she had a flair for emotive figures, which made her a good choice for memorial work.

Another of her memorial works is a bust, cast in 1928, of a British airman of World War One. The style of the flying helmet and the archetypal features suggest the portrait is more of a symbol of the brave pilots of the Royal Flying Corps and Royal Air Force than of any individual. It is possible that she had first-hand knowledge of the pilots of London Colney nearby and she would certainly have been aware of their daring exploits. There is also a bust by Mary Bromet of 'Councillor Mellor' in Bushey Museum. Mary died in Oxhey in 1937.

Bushey and Rickmansworth

Bushey and Rickmansworth possess their own distinguished monumental war memorials and the important Scottish sculptor Sir William Reid Dick, RA (1879–1961), himself a war veteran who had served in France and Palestine, designed both. Amongst his many notable commissions, Sir William worked on a number of other memorials, including the Arras Memorial and the Menin Gate Memorial at Ypres, which were unveiled by Field Marshal Frederick Rudolph Lambart, 10th Earl of Cavan. Lambart was a career soldier and distinguished general of the Great War who, prior to 1914, had been Master of Foxhounds for the Hertfordshire Hunt and resident at Wheathampstead House, Wheathampstead. In 1928 he became Colonel of the Bedfordshire and Hertfordshire Regiment and on retirement a Deputy Lieutenant of Hertfordshire.

The Bushey War Memorial, situated at the junction of Sparrows Herne and School Lane, is an imposing work that features a large sculptured figure of a woman on a plinth in front of a cenotaph, all in Portland stone. The figure is depicted in an attitude of mourning, standing with her head bowed and supported by her left hand. In her right hand she holds a laurel wreath.

For British artists of the period working in the classical style, Peace took the conventional form of a female figure holding aloft an olive branch, palm frond or, occasionally, a dove, but it rarely appears alone. It is more usually presented as a junior partner to the more strident figure of Victory, and located at a lower point on the pedestal arrangement. Sometimes the figure of Peace was shown holding a wreath in both hands as an emblem of a 'Peace Victory won through Service and Sacrifice'.

The popular inscription *Invicta Pax* is similarly ambiguous in that it could mean 'undefeated in war', 'undefeated by death' or even 'peace to the undefeated'. Few, if any, war memorials celebrated peace in its own right. As Alex King, author of *Memorials of the Great War in Britain*, has pointed out, British memorial sculpture implied that Peace was the consequence of Victory, and not an ideal worth promoting as a separate or distinct entity.

The symbolism of the wreath may be ambiguous, representing either the olive wreath of peace or the laurel of victory. The figure is clothed in loose robes and sandals, implying a classical pedigree. The dates '1914' and '1918' are carved in relief on either side of the figure and the inscription is on the opposite side of the cenotaph.

The same figure was used for a private memorial on the Western Front at Givenchy-de-la-Bassee, to Lt. H.G.E. Hill-Trevor, 1st

Bushey War Memorial.

Battalion Scots Guards, who was killed in action on 21 December 1914. The memorial was unveiled on Sunday, 12 March 1922. Dick's design won a competition, but his winning entry was rejected by popular outcry and another design, also by him, was substituted. Lucy Kemp-Welch had also submitted a proposal for a monument for 'Bushey, Bushey Heath and Bushey Grove'. Preliminary sketches for her monument in bronze or stone feature an imposing, draped, female classical figure on a plinth, with two urns on either side where the Watford Memorial has figures.

Today the memorial commemorates the 157 who fell during the Great War and the eighty lost in the Second World War, and bears the inscription:

> *Tranquil you lie, your knightly virtue proved,*
> *Your memory hallowed in the land you loved*

The lines are from a poem to the fallen, 'O Valiant Hearts', by Sir John Stanhope Arkwright, published in *The Supreme Sacrifice, and other Poems in Time of War* (1919). From 1925 onwards the words were also used for a hymn, after being set to music by Vaughan Williams and Gustav Holst, but most popularly by Dr Charles Harris.

The Rickmansworth War Memorial, now sited at St Mary's Church, Church Street, was originally at the Junction of Uxbridge Road and Ebury Road; it was relocated to make way for a roundabout. The Cenotaph was sculpted in Portland stone with a bronze figure, which has now been lost. It has a seated woman at the north and south faces, one symbolizing the sorrow and despair of 1914, and the other the hopeful triumph of 1918.

Dick originally designed the memorial with a pyramid cap on top, but this design was amended to include the statue of a lion with its paws holding down an eagle. The statue was later removed and a pyramid cap substituted in June 1968. The lion and the eagle are now in the public gardens behind the Three Rivers Council Offices. There are 194 names from the Great War and eighty-two from the Second World War. The inscription reads, 'In proud and grateful memory of men of this district who gave their lives in the Great War.'

Rickmansworth War Memorial today. (Photo by Bob Speel)

'Sorrow and Despair 1914' – 'Hope and Victory 1918' (Photo by Bob Speel)

'Hope and Victory 1918' .(Photo by Bob Speel)

Private Commemoration and Private Memorials

Despite the public commemorations, there was still a need for individuals and groups to recognise the contribution of family members, friends and colleagues. On a very private level, memorials could be placed in the home, often consisting of a wooden panel displaying medals. A good example is held in the Bushey Museum, which was created by the Drake family.

Public buildings might house rolls of honour for the wider locality, but they too chose to remember their own, as did work places and factories, schools and communal bodies. Twenty-two staff members from Leavesden Hospital died on active service. In 1958, the framed memorial scroll in the Chapel was replaced by a marble tablet in the entrance hall. Kent's Brushes, the manufacturers of Fine Art paintbrushes at Apsley, had its own memorial of seventeen names on a wooden plaque, which has now been re-sited in the new workshop. The nearby Home Park Paper Mill memorial records thirteen former employees killed.

The long lists of those who gave their lives from The Post Office, Watford Printers and Benskins Brewery are inscribed on rolls of honour now held in the Watford Museum. The Post Office War Memorial was originally above the door in the main Post Office in Market Street, in the centre of Watford. The quiet of the church though, was a natural location for a more contemplative show of grief.

St Mary the Virgin Parish Church, Watford

There are a number of memorials in the Church of St Mary the Virgin, including one from the Boy Scouts:

In Honoured Memory
of
The Old Scouts of the
1ˢᵗ S.W. Herts Troop
Who Fell in the Great War

John C. Heather.
William A Newell.
Philip E. Posner.
Frederick B. Wild
1914 —— 1918

'Who Dies if England Live'

A large memorial is dedicated to the Lake brothers, who were both killed in the same year. John Stephen Raymond Lake, who worked in the Stock Exchange, was a Captain in the South Wales Borderers and had previously served in the South African War. He was wounded at Ypres in 1914 and was killed at Calonne, France on 16 June 1916 and is buried at Calonne Military Cemetery. Reginald St George Lake, also a banker, was a Lieutenant of the 1st Battalion of the Oxfordshire and Buckinghamshire Light Infantry and a member of the Harts Militia. He was killed in Martinpuch, France on 17 November 1916 and buried at the British Cemetery by the men from his own platoon.

St Matthew Parish Church, Oxhey
The Warneford Tablet commemorates Reginald Warneford VC, the pilot who had shot down a Zeppelin over France (see Chapter 1) and under the west window two plaques commemorate John Richard Gutteridge Smith of Wiggenhall and Eric Lillywhite Lailey, both killed in 1916. Outside in the porch is a marble tablet to John MacDonald and Frank Martin, bell-ringers, who also lost their lives.

In the south aisle of the church there is brass dedicated by the Watford Belgian Refugees Committee to the memory of Vera Smith, a Sunday School teacher, who died aged 28 'in recognition of her labours for the unfortunate Belgians during the Great War ... She was for 10 years a Sunday School Teacher and her noble example and sweet disposition won the hearts of all who came in contact with her'. A window, inscribed 'A War Memorial 1914-1918', given by the Girls' Guild of St Cecilia depicts their patron saint, whilst another of 'The Risen Christ' was created in memory of Noel Montague Charles Dudley, aged nineteen, who was killed on the Somme in 1916.

St Peter's Church, Bushey Heath
St Peter's is blessed with some of the most outstanding war memorials to be found in a parish church. The Great West Window is dedicated to the memory of Lieutenant Basil Parrin Hicks, who joined the Inns of Court Officer Training Corps at the outbreak of war and was made a Lieutenant in the Berkshire Regiment. He served with the BEF in France and Flanders and was killed in action at Hulluch on 25 September 1915, while leading the scout section of his battalion in the first attack on Loos. Buried where he fell, Hicks's body was later

The Great West Window. (Courtesy of St Peter's Church, Bushey Heath).

exhumed and re-interred at Dud Corner Military Cemetery, Loos. Worshipped by his men, a private who was with him when he was killed recalled, 'He was a game one. He fell right on the German parapet, his last words being "Good lads, come on, straight ahead!"'

Chapel of St George. (Courtesy of St Peter's Church, Bushey Heath)

Basil Hicks was the younger son of William Mitchinson Hicks, the founding Vice-Chancellor and Professor of Physics at Sheffield University. The Hicks Building at the University is named after him and he also inaugurated the Basil Perrin Hicks Memorial Lecture.

The Great West Window is a reminder of Bushey's artistic connections too. William Hicks had married Ellen Perrin, whose elder brother Henry was married to Ida Southwell Robins. Ida was a talented artist and sculptress. Around 1905 Ida and her husband purchased The Cottage on Bushey Heath, where she opened The De Morgan Pottery Works, named after the famous designer.

As part of the congregation of St. Peter's, Ida's husband Henry served on the Building Committee for the rebuild project started in 1911 and he donated a considerable sum to the work. The new West Window in the enlarged nave was initially in plain glass but when Basil Hicks died, the Perrins commissioned Henry Holiday, RA, to design stained glass for the window depicting Love, Wisdom, Power, Joy, Truth and Faith in memory of their nephew. Holiday was a well-respected painter and designer in the Pre-Raphaelite manner, whose stained glass adorns numerous churches, including Westminster Abbey. Named The Holy Spirit Window it was dedicated before the end of the war on Sunday, 14 April 1918. The glass was made by Lowndes and Drury at the Glasshouse, Fulham.

Roll of Honour. (Courtesy of St Peter's Church, Bushey Heath)

After the War, a memorial chapel was built by public subscription to remember the other members of the church who had sacrificed their lives.

The Foundation Stone was laid on 3 July 1921, by General Phipps Hornby CB CMG, who had won a Victoria Cross in the Boer War. Dedicated to St George and named 'The Warriors' Chapel', it was designed by Fellowes Prynne as an addition on the south side of the chancel, with stained glass windows and in the same style as the main building. It contains the parish war memorial.

The two groups of three windows above the war memorial were donated by members of the congregation. The designs were the work

Window with Saints Alban, Andrew and Martin:

Alban – in memory of David & Macfie Keith Johnston RNAS 1915.

Andrew – given by the congregation. Armistice Day 1923.

Martin – given by the congregation. Patronal Festival 1924.

(Courtesy of St Peter's Church, Bushey Heath)

Window depicting the Saints Patrick, George and David:

Patrick – given by mothers George – given by comrades. David – 'in memory of David Angus. Gibbs aged 19. Somme 1918.'

(Courtesy of St Peter's Church, Bushey Heath)

of the Percy Bacon Brothers of the British Society of Master Glass Painters.

St Mary the Virgin Parish Church, Rickmansworth

St Mary the Virgin's former Vicar, Alfred Edward Northey (1838–1911), had two sons serving in the army during the Great War. William Brook MC was a Major in the Gurkha Rifles and he wrote several books about the Gurkhas and Nepal. Lieutenant Alfred Northey, was a regular officer of the Royal Worcestershire Regiment. He was killed in action in France on 12 October 1914, aged twenty-eight, and was buried at Brown's Road Military Cemetery, Festubert. A fine octagonal stone font was given in his memory.

Aftermath

On the morning of Monday, 11 November 1918, the news of the Armistice was greeted by the sounding of every hooter and siren in the area. The factories closed for the day and bunting appeared on Watford streets which thronged with celebrating crowds. Once again the lights shone brightly in the marketplace.

The *Watford News* was pleased to report that, despite young people giving vent to their feelings, there was singing into the night but no rowdyism. The Deputy Chief Constable was able to inform the magistrates the next day that there had not been a single case of drunkenness or disorderly conduct. Church services of thanksgiving were held. In Bushey the celebrations had been muted, however, as the village was in the throes of the flu epidemic, with a number of fatalities.

The war had cost the British Army 673,375 personnel recorded as dead and missing, with another 1,643,469 wounded as the result of enemy action and disease. The rush to demobilise at the end of the war substantially decreased the strength of the army, from its peak of 4,000,000 men in 1918 to 370,000 men by 1920.

Local Peace Day celebrations were held the next summer, on 19 July. In Cassiobury Park, there were processions, music, dancing and games and in Hemel Hempstead the Council splashed out £50 on decorations. In Chorleywood a short church service was followed by processions and tea for the children (every child receiving a commemorative mug), with a conjurer and ventriloquist supplied by Sir Henry Wood, the inaugurator of the Albert Hall promenade concerts, who lived locally. There were also a variety of entertainments: races, games, wrestling on horseback, dancing, a supper, an open-air concert and finally fireworks.

It took some time for official war memorials to be built, but

Peace celebrations dinner held in Watford on 19 July 1919. (Hertfordshire Archives).

Peace celebrations on 19 July 1919, in Cassiobury Park. (Hertfordshire Archives).

Remembrance Day parades soon became an annual feature of British life, held in every town and village, accompanied by the laying of wreaths. Ten years after the beginning of the war an open air Armistice Day service was held outside the Watford Council office in 1924, with a two-minute silence.

In order that the terror of the 'war to end all wars' was not repeated, the Watford Branch of the League of Nations Union took an active role in trying to prevent a second conflict. Remembrance Day parades were used as a focus for anti-war demonstrations organised in 1935, following the Italian invasion of Abyssinia.

The aftermath of the War was also dominated by the authorities' attempts to fulfil the promise to the returning soldiers that they would come back to a 'home fit for heroes'. Though the social welfare changes interrupted by the War gathered pace afterwards, heralding a 'Brave New World' of modernity, wartime austerity did not cease straight away and hardships continued. The shortage of gas meant that Hemel Hempstead's streetlights remained unlit for some time. There was also high unemployment and wages remained low. Lack of housing was an immediate problem, and the Government encouraged the building of houses for ex-servicemen and key workers, with local schemes inaugurated throughout the area. New housing projects began in Watford as soon as land became available. Transport links were improved too, but people in Watford and Bushey were once again wary of being swallowed up by Greater London.

Ex-soldiers replaced women war workers in many jobs, but the previous gendered definition of their roles had been eroded. After the introduction of the new Representation of the People Act by Lloyd George, the General Election of December 1918 was the first in which all men over the age of 21 and women over 30 who met minimum property qualifications could vote. The Coalition swept to a landslide victory; the day of the Labour Party had not yet arrived. In April 1919, the first woman councillor, Mrs Amy Wheelwright, was elected to Bushey Urban District Council.

A further sign of change was the demise of Cassiobury House, for so long the symbol of local prestige and power. George Devereux de Vere Capell, the 7th Earl of Essex died in 1916 and the house was left empty. After the war, Lady Essex was obliged to sell up to pay the death duties and it was then demolished for its materials in 1927. Other large houses and estates were also sold and broken up, and the gentry lost its grip on local affairs. The Grove, the former home of Lord Clarendon, became a gardening school in the 1920s, then subsequently a health centre, riding school, girls' boarding school and finally a golf club and hotel. Ashridge Park where the Territorials were training on the eve of the War was taken over in part by the National Trust in 1921, while the remainder became a Golf Club and the House a 'College of Citizenship' for the Conservative Party, part of Charing Cross Hospital in World War II and finally a Business School.

The munitions factories quickly became available for peacetime use, leading to the introduction of new industries. HM No. 1 Munitions Works became Penfold Fencing and part of the Co-operative (demolished 1985). In January 1919, the *Watford Observer* reported that the Government was selling a thirty-three acre factory site comprising 124,000 sq ft of buildings which had housed a 'projectile factory', referring to HM No. 2.

In 1926, when the Greycaine Book Manufacturing Company moved to Watford it took over a twenty-acre site in Bushey Mill Lane, near Watford North Railway Station, which contained some large wooden buildings formerly used for munitions manufacture and a railway siding connecting with the main line to Euston. The wooden buildings were quickly replaced with sturdier, less flammable structures, an indictment of the safety levels at the old Filling Works. The Watford Manufacturing Company, makers of Dr Tibbles' Cocoa at the Victoria Works reverted from munitions to peacetime production as well, but following a period of over-investment the company went bankrupt in 1922.

Despite their fears, at the start of the war the Cobra works in Bushey survived. The parent company Blyth and Platt also had a factory in Sidney Australia where their adverts in *The Sydney Bulletin*, featuring a character named 'Chunder Loo of Akim Foo'. He proved so popular that a book was published in 1916 entitled, *The Adventures of Chunder Loo*. The character's name, often abbreviated to Chunder, became a nickname during the war. It has been surmised that the use of Chunder Loo, as rhyming slang for 'spew' was the origin of the word 'chunder'. Blyth & Platt Ltd. was bought out by Chiswick Products Ltd. in 1928. Production at the Cobra works continued until the company closed in 1953.

The end of the war also saw the completion of the consolidation of the print industry with, Ashworth, Meredith & Downer Ltd., Geo. Jones Ltd, (renamed Menpes Printing and Engraving), whose sizeable works in Whipendell Road was built in 1906, and the Bushey Colour Press, all becoming part of Sun Engraving Co. Ltd., employing 300 workers.

The shortcomings of local public services had been highlighted during the war. For example, the Peace Memorial Wing of Watford General Hospital came about when the local hospital was discovered to be inadequate for the treatment of the war wounded. The wing, costing £90,000, was opened by the Princess Royal, Princess Mary in 1925, built by funds raised by public appeal.

Not only did the fabric of life have to be stitched together again, but also the damage to human lives would take time to heal. Created in the 1930s, Macdonnell Gardens in Watford was a purpose-built development of bungalows for disabled ex-military officers, featuring a central green with memorial gardens and a flag. Old soldiers rekindled comradeship and memories in Old Comrades and regimental veterans' associations and local branches of the British Legion were founded. The Comrades of the Great War Club, at the British Legion headquarters in St Albans Road, was opened in 1919.

These forms of memorial and closure, however poignant at the time, proved not to be the final chapter, as world war would be repeated a mere generation later. Neither expectation of a further war nor extensive commemoration was in the minds of those who gave their lives during the Great War. In the words of the war poet Edmund Blunden:

At that period above all, the soldier felt that his death would be his complete and final disappearance.

Bibliographical Note

A number of different sources were consulted during the research for this book. The Introduction owes much to the Hertfordshire Archives & Local Studies, as well as to the Victoria County History, company and other business records. For Parliamentary Papers we consulted *Hansard*, while the *London Gazette* has helped us confirm gallantry awards.

For local reportage we relied mainly on the *Watford Observer* and the *Watford Illustrated*, a paper founded to deal with the need for war news, but we have also drawn on smaller papers.

We also consulted the many meticulously produced publications of individual parish churches, in addition to local historical and architectural/archaeological societies in our 'catchment area', an area of geographical and historical distinctiveness and unity which roughly follows the distribution area of the *Watford Observer*, with the exclusion of Middlesex.

We also benefited from the knowledge recorded in the following PhD theses:

- Ilana Ruth Bet-El, 'Experience into identity: the writings of British conscript soldiers, 1916–1918', PhD Thesis, UCL, 1991

- David Monger, 'The National War Aims Committee and British patriotism during the First World War', PhD Thesis, Kings College London, 2009

- David Fowler Summers, 'The Labour church and allied movements of the late 19th and early 20th centuries', PhD Thesis, University of Edinburgh, 1958

The following excellent dissertation by Jean Rannard has been very helpful in outlining the historical geography of the region:

- Jean Rannard, 'The Location and Economic Growth of the Watford Paper and Printing Industries', Unpublished Dissertation, Department of Geography, University of Bristol, 1963

On-going research projects conducted by universities, genealogy societies, sport historians, war commemoration groups and other official, self-governing or grass-roots bodies have enriched our work further. The rest of our information was checked and cross-referenced from published books. All of these debts are recorded in our Bibliography.

We have also used our own long-term knowledge of the region and our own photography for some of the sites we mention. For other images used permissions were sought wherever possible. All uncredited photographs were taken by the authors.

We would particularly like to thank Chris Reynolds of the Hertfordshire Genealogy and author of *The London Gunners come to Town* for his advice, as well as The Isle of Wight History Society and Bob Speel for the use of their pictures. Moreover, we are grateful to Father Andrew Burton, BA, SSC, for permission to use the stunning images of the interior of St Peter's Church, Bushey Heath. We thank the Staff and Volunteers of the Watford and Bushey Museums for their kind assistance and Chris Bennett and Gary Moyle of Hertfordshire Archives and Local Studies (HALS) and the Librarians of Watford Central Library and Bushey Library for permissions and advice on their collections.

Bibliography

A History of the Parish Church of St Mary the Virgin, Rickmansworth, St Mary's, Rickmansworth, 2006

Adie, Kate, *Fighting on the Home Front: the Legacy of Women in World War One,* Hodder, London, 2013

Anderson, Henry, 'Fullerians of WWI and WWW2' and 'The Fallen of Watford Grammar School for Boys', in G. Aitken (ed.), *The Fullerian 2013 – 14*, Watford Grammar School for Boys, 2014

Bard, Robert, *Elstree and Borehamwood through Time,* Amberley Publishing, Stroud, 2011

Barham, Peter, *Forgotten Lunatics of the Great War*, New Haven, CT, Yale University Press, 2004

Beerbohm, Max, *Letters to Reggie Turner*, Rupert Hart-Davis, London, 1964

Bennewith, Walter, B.D., *The Beechen Grove Story: a history of Beechen Grove Bapstist Church, Watford*, B.G. Press, Watford, 1983

Bet-El, Ilana Ruth, 'Experience into identity: the writings of British conscript soldiers, 1916–1918', PhD, University College London, 1991

Blunden, Edmund, 'Introduction', in Fabian Arthur Goulstone Ware, *The Immortal Heritage: an account of the work and policy of the Imperial war graves commission during twenty years, 1917–1937*, Imperial War Graves Commission, Cambridge University Press, Cambridge, 1937

Brey, Marjery, *Oxhey, History of a Parish,* Oxhey Parochial Church Council, 1979

Briggs, Asa, *A Social History of England,* Weidenfeld and Nicolson, London, 1983

Brooke, Rupert, 'The Old Vicarage, Granchester', 1912

Buckley, Francis, *Q. 6. A and Other Places: Recollections of 1916, 1917, 1918*, Spottiswoode, Ballantyne & Co Ltd, London, 1920

Clark, C.W., *Abbots Langley Then: 1790–1960*, self-published, Hertfordshire, 1997

Come to Hertfordshire: Official Guide, Simmath Press, Dundee, 1948

Conder, Eustace R., *Josiah Conder: A Memoir*, London, 1857

Cornell, Martyn, 'Benskins of Watford', *Brewery History,* No. 110, Winter 2002, pp. 9 - 15

Crane, David, *Empires of the Dead: How One Man's Vision Led to the Creation of WWI War Graves*, William Collins, London, 2013

Defoe, Daniel, *Tour thro' the whole Island of Great Britain, vol. 2,* London, 1761

Diplock, Monica, *The History of Leavesden Hospital*, Abbots Langley, 1990

Fish, Jack, *Notes on the History of Hemel Hempstead Bowls Club*, Hemel Hempstead Bowls Club, 2010

Hansard, Volumes 58–105, 1914–18, Her Majesty's Stationery Office

Hunns, Terry, *Watford: Extensive Urban Survey Project Report*, Watford, 2000

Johnson, W.B., *Industrial Archaeology of Hertfordshire*, London, 1970

Jones, Ira, *King of Airfighters: The Biography of Major Mick Mannock, VC, DSO MC,* Casemate Publishers, 2009

King George's Recreation Ground: Celebrating 100 Years (Leaflet), Hertsmere Borough Council, 2012

King, Alex, *Memorials of the Great War in Britain: The Symbolism and Politics of Remembrance*, Bloomsbury, London, 2014

Knight, Judith, *Watford*, The Archive Photographs Series, Chalford, Stroud, 1995

Lloyd George, David, *War Memoirs, Vol. 1,* Nicholson & Watson, London, 1933

MacDonagh, Michael, *In London during the Great War: The diary of a journalist,* Eyre and Spottiswoode, London, 1935

Mackersey, Ian, *No Empty Chairs The Short and Heroic Lives of the Young Aviators Who Fought and Died in the First World War*, Weidenfeld & Nicolson, London, 2012

Messenger, Charles, *Terriers in the Trenches: The Post Officer Rifles at War 1914–1918*, Picton Publishing, Chippenham, 1982

Mills, Barry, 'The Achievements and Limitations of the Northern Friends Peace Board 1913–20', Peace History Conference, Manchester, 2013

Monger, David, 'The National War Aims Committee and British patriotism during the First World War', PhD Thesis, Kings College London, 2009

Moorhouse, Paul, *The Great War in Portraits*, with an essay by Sebastian Faulks, National Gallery Publications, London, 2014

Murphey, Janet, *Bushey during the Great War, 1914–1918*, Bushey Museum Trust, Bushey, 2009

Nationally Listed Buildings in Watford, Watford Borough Council, 2014

Nunn, Bob (ed), *The Book of Watford: a portrait of our town, c. 1800–1987*, Pageprint, Watford, 1987

Oxford Dictionary of Biography

Page, William (ed.), 'Watford Introduction', *A History of the County of Hertford: volume 2,* Victoria County History, 1908, (pp. 446–451, 'Watford Manors', pp. 451–464; 'Parishes: Bushey', pp. 179-186, 'Hemel Hempstead', pp. 215–230, King's Langley', pp. 234–245, 'Abbot's Langley', pp. 323–328, 'Aldenham', pp. 149–161, 'Shenley', pp. 254–273, 'Elstree', pp. 349–351, 'Rickmansworth', pp. 371–386, 'Sarratt', pp. 438–443)

Parker, David, *Hertfordshire Children in War and Peace: 1914–1939,* Hertfordshire Publications, Hatfield, 2007

Parkin, Bryon, *St. Peter's, the Church on the Heath: an illustrated history 1836–2004,* Bushey Museum Trust, Bushey, 2004

Parkin, Bryon, *The Arts and Crafts of Bushey Heath*, Bushey Museum Trust, Bushey, 2003

Parrish, Ted, *Echoes of Old Watford, Bushey and Oxhey*, Past Days, Charmouth, 2013

Pearsall, Ronald, *Edwardian Life and Leisure*, Newton Abbot, 1995

Penwarden, Alan, *Home Park Paper Mill at King's Langley*, Hertfordshire, Apsley, 2011

Phillips, Oliver, *Watford in the 20th century*, Volume 1 (1900–1939), Watford Observer, Watford, 2011

Planning Policy Team, *Watford Character of Area Study,* Watford Borough Council, 2011

Plummer, Steve J., *The Wheelwright Family Story,* Cloth Wrap, 2010

Rannard, Jean, 'The Location and Economic Growth of the Watford Paper and Printing Industries', Unpublished Dissertation, Department of Geography, University of Bristol, 1963

Revell, Alex, *Aviation Elite Unites: No 56 Sqn RAF/RFC*, Osprey Publishing, Oxford, 2009

Ray, George E., *The Book of Chorleywood & Chenies,* Barracuda Books, Buckingham, 1983

Reynolds, Bertha and Chris, *The London Gunners come to Town: Life and Death in Hemel Hempstead in the Great War*, CODIL Language Systems in association with the Dacorum Heritage Trust, Tring, 1995

Robinson, Gwennah, *Hertfordshire: Barracuda Guide to County History*, Vol. III, Barracuda Books, Chesham, 1978

Sainsbury, J.D., *Hertfordshire Soldiers from 1787*, Hitchin, Local History Council, 1969

Sainsbury, J.D., *A Biographical List of Officers of the Hertfordshire Yeomanry, 1794–1920*, Hart Books, Welwyn, 2004

Saunders, W.R., *History of Watford*, S.R. Publishers Limited, Watford, 1970; original edition published by C.H. Peacock, Ltd., Watford, 1931

Scleater, Ian, *The Story of the Palace Theatre Watford,* Atlantic Publishing, Rickmansworth, 2008

Seal, Graham, *The Soldiers' Press: Trench Journals in the First World War,* Palgrave Macmillan, Basingstoke, 2013

St. Andrews Church, Watford 1857–1957, 1957

Stamp, Gavin, 'Lost Lululand', *Apollo Magazine*, 28 November 2008

Summers, David Fowler, 'The Labour church and allied movements of the late 19th and early 20th centuries', PhD Thesis, University of Edinburgh, 1958

Summers, Julie, *British and Commonwealth War Cemeteries*, Osprey, London, 2010

Talbot, Mike and Mary (eds), *Talbotania, Journal of the Talbot Research Organisation*, vol. 16, no. 3, Oct 2003, p. 74

Watford Official Town Guide, 1967

Watford War Assistance Committee Report (1921)

Watford: a Pictorial Guide, Borough of Watford, 1951

Wiggins, June, *Abbots Hill School, 1912–2012: celebrating one hundred years of memories*, self-published, 2012

Wolmar, Christian, *Fire and Steam: a new history of the railways in Britain*, Atlantic, London, 2009

Zeepvat, Bob, ''Nash Mills *The Endless Web* Revisited', *Industrial Archaeology Review*, XXXII, I, 2010 pp. 46–62

Records and Archives

Hertfordshire Archives & Local Studies

'John Dickinson and Co. Ltd.', Hertfordshire Archive and Local Studies, GB 0046 D/Edi, 1998

Modern Records Centre, University Library, University of Warwick

The National Archives:

Barnes, Chris and David Langrish, 'Appealing against conscription? Not just for conscientious objectors', 2012: http//blog-nationalarchives.gov.uk

'Defence of the Realm Consolidation Act, 27 November 1914', MUN 5/19/221/8 (Nov 1914)

The Munitions of War Act, 1915

Newspapers and Periodicals

'A Divine Comedy of Watford', *Socialist Standard,* May 1916

Harrogate Herald, September 1917

Herts Advertiser, July 1916

London Gazette

Round the Circuit, Wesleyan Methodist Magazine, 1919

St Peter's Press: the Magazine of St Peter's Church, Bushey Heath (Monthly except January and August), Bushey Museum, 1950 to the present

The Daily Telegraph

The Times

Watford Illustrated, 1914–1916

Watford Observer

Websites

Anon, 'An Aviator', Bromet (Exh 1889–1932), Bonhams Auction 2011: www.bonhams.com/auctions/18544/lot/727

Anon, 'Connecting up a diverse town: Watford Junction' (Watford Borough Council): www.watfordjunction.org.uk

Anon, 'Herts at War', North Hertfordshire District Council, 2014: www.hertsatwar.co.uk/belgian-refugees

Anon, 'Mary, Pownall (Bromet)', *Mapping the Practice and Profession of Sculpture in Britain and Ireland 1851–1951*, University of Glasgow: http://sculpture.gla.ac.uk/view/person.php?id=msib5_1210004966

Anon, 'The Long Trail': www.1914-1918.net/brothersdied.htm

Anon, 'The military hospitals at home', *The Long Trail: The British Army in the Great War of 1914-1918:* www.19141918.net/hospitals_uk.htm

Bevan, Dai, *Roll of Honour: Hertfordshire*, 2008: www.roll-of-honour.com/Hertfordshire

Boden, Anthony, 'Ivor Gurney: A Biographical outline' , The Ivor Gurney Society: http://ivorgurney.org.uk/biography.htm

Bourne, John, Centre for First World War Studies: www.birmingham.ac.uk/research/activity/warstudies/research/projects/lionsdonkeys/index.aspx

British Boxing History: www.boxinghistory.org.uk/records/50839-Phil-Horwood-Watford.pdf

Cathedral and Abbey Church of Saint Alban: www.stalbanscathedral.org/history

Chorleywood Parish Council: www.chorleywood-pc.gov.uk/war-memorial-hall.html

Commonwealth War Graves Commission: www.cwgc.org

'Death of a Zeppelin, 1916,' EyeWitness to History: www.eyewitnesstohistory.com (2005)

English Heritage; http://list.englishheritage.org.uk/resultsingle.aspx?uid=1001649

Epsom and Ewell History Explorer: www.epsomandewellhistoryexplorer.org.uk/Northeys4.html

Find a Grave: www.findagrave.com ; www.findagrave.com/cgi-bin/fg.cgi?page=gr&GScid=1723620&GRid=75057245&; http://albertball.homestead.com

Francis, Paul, *First World War – Ministry of Munitions and Munitions Factories*:
www.airfieldinformationexchange.org/community/showthread.php
?11695-FIRST-WORLD-WAR-Ministry-of-Munitions-and-
Munitions-Factories;

Gough, Paul, 'Can peace be set in stone?' *Times Higher Education Supplement*: www.timeshighereducation.co.uk/features/can-peace-
be-set-in-stone/175809.article

Grace's Guide: British Industrial History: www.gracesguide.co.uk

'Heritage and History Projects', Hertfordshire Hub, University of
Hertfordshire: www.herts.ac.uk/heritage-hub

Hertfordshire Genealogy: www.hertfordshire-genealogy.co.uk;
http://hertfordshire-genealogy.blogspot.co.uk

Herts Past Policing: Wiseman, Andy, 'Men of the Hertfordshire
Constabulary go to war':
www.hertspastpolicing.org.uk/page/men_of_the_hertfordshire_con
stabulary_go_to_war?path=0p34p

Higginbotham, Peter, 'The Workhouse: the story of an institution':
www.workhouses.org.uk/Watford

History of Radlett Cricket Club, history.radlettcc.com/1910s/1919:
http://heritagehub.herts.ac.uk/projects/airfields.htm

Jones, Robert, 'Lewis Jones: A Biography', 2012:
www.mooch.org.uk/serious

Martin, Cyril, *Park Street's Past:* www.riverver.co.uk/memories-
pdfs/ParkStreet.pdf

National Archives, 'The anti-war movement':
www.nationalarchives.gov.uk/pathways/firstworldwar/spotlights/an
tiwar.htm

Outline History of the British Railway Network:
http://myweb.tiscali.co.uk/gansg/1-hist/01hist.htm

Reveley, Mike, 'Jack Scott, 1902–1986', Kings Langley History and
Museum Society, 1980: www.kingslangley.org.uk/JackScott.html

Scarlet Finders (War Hospital Supply Depots):
www.scarletfinders.co.uk/178.html

Shenley Village Cricket Club History:
http://shenleycc.hitscricket.com/history/default.aspx

Shrimpton, Sue, 'Watford Isolation Hospital', West Watford History:
www.westwatfordhistorygroup.org/isolationhospital.htm

St Albans and Hertfordshire Architectural and Archaeological
   Society: www.stalbanshistory.org
St Matthew's Church, Oxhey:
   www.stmatthewsoxhey.org.uk/memorials.html
St Peter's Church, Bushey Heath:
   www.stpeterbusheyheath.org.uk/section/30
The Drill Hall Project: www.drillhalls.org
The History of Sun Engraving and Sun Printers:
   www.sunprintershistory.com (2014)
The Lost Hospitals of London (2014):
   http://ezitis.myzen.co.uk/briefhistoryauxhosps.html
The Music Hall and Theatre History Website:
   www.arthurlloyd.co.uk/WatfordPalaceTheatre.htm
The Unofficial Reading FC Statistics Site:
   www.royalsrecord.co.uk/seasons/1915.html#WL
The Watford Football Club Archive: www.watfordfcarchive.com
The Women's Land Army:
   www.womenslandarmy.co.uk/tag/hertfordshire
Waterson, Jill, 'The Greycaine Book Manufacturing Company':
   www.history-pieces.co.uk (2011)
Waterson, Jill, 'Leavesden Road, Watford, 1901': www.history-
   pieces.co.uk (2008)

Index

Page numbers in italics denote pictures in the text